Model Railway
Locomotive
Building
on the Cheap!
Volume 2

• SILVER LINK LIBRARY OF RAILWAY MODELLING •

Model Railway Locomotive Building on the Cheap!
Volume 2

**An alternative to kit-building –
how to convert ready-to-run models into
unavailable classes or unusual variants**

K. Chadwick

Silver Link Publishing Ltd

First published in 2008

British Library Cataloguing in Publication Data

A catalogue record for this book is available from the British Library.

ISBN 978 1 85794 312 2

Silver Link Publishing Ltd
The Trundle
Ringstead Road
Great Addington
Kettering
Northants NN14 4BW

Tel/Fax: 01536 330588
email: sales@nostalgiacollection.com
Website: www.nostalgiacollection.com

Printed and bound in the Czech Republic

All photographs are by the author unless otherwise credited.

The author is grateful to the suppliers of parts used in the building of these locomotives, which were available at the time of writing.

Historical notes were compiled with the assistance of the RCTS 'Green Bible'.

A Silver Link book
from
The NOSTALGIA *Collection*

Modelspares and East Kent Models can supply spare parts (including unpainted body-shells) at reasonable cost. For example, at the time of writing the LNER 'B17' body seen here cost £4.00.

CONTENTS

PREFACE

When Silver Link requested material for this second volume, I was quite surprised – the first volume must have been successful! I would therefore first like to thank all those who purchased copies of Volume 1, in spite of criticism in certain quarters – 'Your model of a "D20" doesn't have the correct number of rivets along the base of the smokebox' or 'The wheels on your model of the "C2X" don't have the correct number of spokes.' So some people do actually count rivets and spokes on models! All I can say is that building an engine of your own gives you a great deal of pleasure and satisfaction, and as far as the rivet-and-spoke-counters are concerned the hobby of railway modelling belongs to 'us muddlers' just as much as it does to the 'experts'.

Also, the conversion of ready-to-run models into other locos can save quite a lot of money as long as you are willing to accept a little 'modeller's licence'. For example, the ex-S&DJR 7F 2-8-0 project in Volume 1, constructed from various available Hornby bodies, Plasticard and a variety of detailing parts, came out at just under £100. By contrast, the cost of a proprietary loco kit, set of wheels, motor, detailing parts and the services of a professional model loco builder would have been a little over £350.

Furthermore, my conversions, utilising ready-to-run chassis, will negotiate second-radius curves and small-radius pointwork. I remember talking to a professional model loco builder some time ago on the subject of an LNER 'B16'. He said, 'A "B16" to negotiate second-radius curves? Impossible! Forget it! The wheelbase is too long.' Well, my conversion (although very complicated, and not a project for the faint-hearted), described in this volume, does just that.

Now for a change of subject. On my travels I have met many modellers who are dubious about soldering. My advice to them is to have a go and learn by your mistakes. ('He who makes no mistakes usually doesn't make anything', as the saying goes, and 'A fool who persists in his folly may in time become wise'!) Although it pays in the long run to invest in a really good-quality soldering-iron, when I first started I bought cheap things that only seemed to last 5 minutes. Eventually I bought an Antex soldering-iron – more expensive, but it has so far lasted 15 years! As regards solder and flux, I use the products of Carr's Modelling Products Ltd, which are of very good quality and I can recommend them. They also produce a *Soldering Handbook*, which would prove very useful.

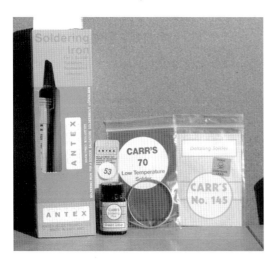

Soldering equipment.

Ex-LNER 'B16/3' 4-6-0 No 61444

One day in the spring of 1964 I was late-turn in the booking-office at Ferriby (NER). To say that I was in a bad mood would have been an understatement – being 16 at the time I had better things to do with my evenings than spending them at work. In addition, I had been informed that my job had been cut out and I was waiting to hear where I would be transferred to. This was not, however, part of the famous (or infamous) 'Beeching Plan', but one of the regular reorganisations that we had on the railways where people at the bottom got cut out and those at the top got promoted even higher! Unfortunately, at this time I only had 12 months' seniority, so I was very much at the bottom of the pile!

At about 16.00 the platform bell rang four times (that meant that the signalman wanted me). I went out on to the platform and Jack Potts, the late-turn signalman, shouted across to me, 'Steam on the fish train!'

The fish-train in question was the 16.09 Hull (West) to King's Cross, which had been in the hands of English Electric Type 3s (Class 37) for some time. Luckily for me the 16.16 local DMU into Paragon was on time and I was able to get out on to the platform in readiness. The plume of white smoke came around the bend in the river between Hessle and Ferriby, and continued towards me at a cracking pace. As it entered the station I recognised the loco as one of Dairycoates's 'B16/3s', No 61444 (this class were always good performers). I continued to watch the train as it swept away westwards and out of sight. Needless to say the spectacle cheered me up quite a lot and the memory remained with me for the next 40-plus years! Which is just as well, for that was the last time I saw a 'B16'; No 61444 was condemned in June 1964, and the very last

one, No 61435, was condemned the following month.

The North Eastern Railway introduced its Class 'S3' 4-6-0 mixed-traffic locomotives in 1919. They were designed by Sir Vincent Raven and employed 5ft 8in-diameter driving wheels, with a 5ft 6in-diameter boiler (as fitted to the Class 'T3' 0-8-0 freight design – LNER Class 'Q7' – which was also introduced to service in 1919). The 'S3' design employed three cylinders, all of which drove on the leading coupled axle, with three separate sets of Stephenson valve-gear, all placed between the frames. A total of 70 locos were built, 38 by the North Eastern and a further 32 by the LNER after the Grouping.

In 1937 Gresley 'modernised' one of the locos (LNER No 2364, BR No 61435) with Walschaerts valve-gear, and outside valve chests, for the outside cylinders, together with his famous 'derived motion' for the inside cylinder. To make way for the 'derived motion' the bogie had to be moved further forward, thus lengthening the rebuilt loco by 12 inches. During this rebuilding the opportunity was taken to fit a more modern cab and raise the running-plate clear of the driving wheels. Six more locos were similarly dealt with, and these seven rebuilds became LNER sub-class 'B16/2' (the original design being designated 'B16/1'). Strangely, in spite of the aforementioned modernising features, the seven 'B16/2' rebuilds were left with the original (and by now 'old-fashioned') right-hand drive.

Between 1944 and 1949 Edward Thompson rebuilt a further 17 locos along similar lines but with left-hand drive and an additional set of Walschaerts valve-gear for the inside cylinder. Unfortunately, due to the lack of maintenance brought about by wartime conditions the

Above 'B16/3' 4-6-0 No 61420 at Hotchley Hill, north of Loughborough, with the 1.07pm Leicester-Annesley freight on 23 July 1962. *David Holmes*

Below The completed model. The locomotive is a bit longer than it should be due to the spacing of the driving wheels, but it looks like what it is supposed to be, and it runs well! The transfers are by Modelmaster, Fox and SMS. (I left the rear sandboxes unpainted so that they would show up for the camera.)

Gresley 'derived motion' had started to give problems and no further locomotives were built with it. Remember the old adage, 'The more complicated a thing is the more there is to go wrong with it'! These 17 Thompson locos became LNER sub-class 'B16/3', and were identical in outward appearance to the Gresley products apart from having the vacuum-ejector pipe and reversing-rod on the left-hand side instead of the right.

One of the original 'B16/1' locos was destroyed in an air-raid in 1942, while the rest of the class (24 rebuilds and 45 originals) survived to become BR property in 1948. Before the Second World War all three sub-classes were mostly confined to ex-NER metals (although some did venture as far south as Doncaster). However, with a large number of locomotives lost to enemy action during the war, members of the class began appearing at King's Cross, Marylebone and even Banbury (on inter-regional workings). These southerly forays continued into the 1950s, but as the new 'B1s' began to be delivered those forays gradually ceased. By the end of 1961 the 'B16/1s' had become extinct and the 24 rebuilds were confined to just three sheds: York (50A), Dairycoates (53A), and Mirfield (56D). The Thompson rebuilds became extinct in June 1964 with the withdrawal of Nos 61418, 61434, 61444, 61448, 61454, 61463 and 61467. The last example of the Gresley variety (No 61435) was withdrawn from service the following month. All three versions of the class were very popular with North Eastern crews, but the ex-LMS men at Mirfield, who were used to locos with Belpaire fireboxes, did not take to them. Round-tops and Belpaires do require different firing techniques, after all!

A model of one of these locos would be a very useful and interesting addition to any LNER-based layout.

Items required

Hornby 'Patriot' loco chassis block (Margate version preferable); 'Patriot' front bogie; pair of *Chinese* coupling-rods for 'Patriot' loco; 'Patriot' tender drawbar; complete set of driving wheels from *Margate* version of Fowler 2-6-4 tank loco (including screws for coupling-rods and valve-gear spacers); Class 'D49' cylinder block and valve-gear; Class 'B17' loco body; complete tender from Class 'B17' or 'D49'; detailing parts described in text.

Stage 1: The loco chassis

The Hornby 'Patriot' has been in production for a long time now, and I am informed by a reliable source that there have been *four* different designs of chassis block during that time (two from Margate, two from China). For my model I used a Chinese version (reference R357), although, as far as I can see, this conversion should still be possible utilising the other versions of the chassis block with slightly different modifications.

First, before fitting the 23mm-diameter driving wheels (from the Fowler 2-6-4 tank), we need to remove the mounting pillar for the tender drawbar, together with a small portion of the front end (in order to fit the 'D49' cylinder block) (see **Figure 1**). Next drill two 10BA (2mm-diameter) holes through the front end of the chassis block to take the 'D49' cylinder block (see **Figure 2**). Then cut out two pieces of card or thin Plasticard and glue them in place on each side of the chassis with their top edges in line with the top of the chassis block (**Figure 3**); these will form an insulating barrier to prevent short-circuits when we fit the 'D49' valve-gear. Finally, if you are using the chassis block from the R357 model, you will need to cover the large gaps in the casting with two pieces of paper 15mm by 12mm, and paint them black before fitting the wheels (see again **Figure 1**).

At this point in the proceedings we can fit the wheels, underframe and coupling-rods. The holes in the Chinese 'Patriot' coupling-rods may need enlarging with a file to fit the fixing screws from the Fowler tank.

With these jobs done, we can now turn our attention to the 'D49' cylinder block. First file (or cut) away the centre 12mm (6mm either side of the centre-line) of the raised ridge on the underside of the cylinder-block (**Figure 4**). Then file (or cut) away the leading inside corners of each cylinder to allow the bogie to swing (again see **Figure 4**). Next force two 10BA screws through the inside ends of the leading 'slots' on

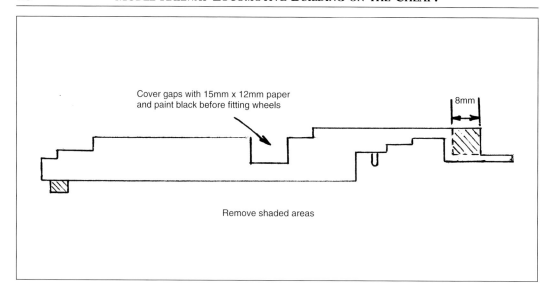

Cover gaps with 15mm x 12mm paper and paint black before fitting wheels

8mm

Remove shaded areas

Above Figure 1: Modifications to 'Patriot' chassis block (R357)

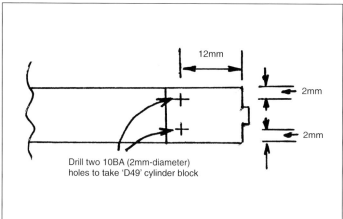

12mm

2mm

2mm

Drill two 10BA (2mm-diameter) holes to take 'D49' cylinder block

Left Figure 2: Holes for positioning cylinders

Below Figure 3: Manufacture and positioning of insulating tabs

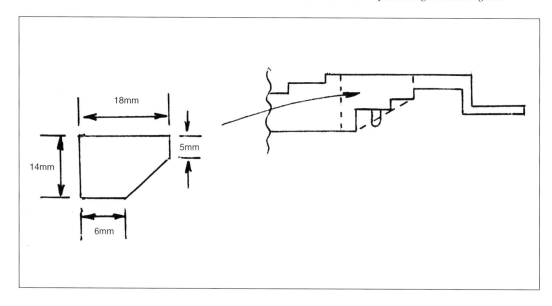

18mm

5mm

14mm

6mm

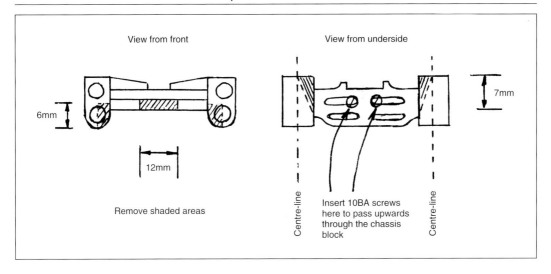

Figure 4: Modifications to cylinder block

the underside of the cylinder block (**Figure 4** again); the metal thread of the screw should cut its way through the plastic. Then thread the screws through the two holes that you drilled earlier through the front end of the chassis block, and secure them in place by fixing a 10BA nut to each screw. Note that the cylinder block is fitted to the underside of the chassis block and the screws are threaded upwards through the assembly with the nuts on the top.

With the cylinders in position we can now move on to the 'D49' valve-gear. On the Hornby 'D49' the motion support brackets fit into recesses in the sides of the chassis block. Unfortunately the 'Patriot' does not have these recesses, so we need to bend the innermost 5mm of each support bracket forwards through 90° so that the valve-gear will fit. When you've got the valve-gear fitted in place, glue a small piece of microstrip to each 'insulating tab' (which you fitted earlier) directly underneath the end of each support bracket, thus preventing any downward movement.

Assuming that the driving wheels rotate freely without any 'binding' of the valve-gear, we can move on to the front bogie. First remove the original 'Patriot' swing-link by drilling out the rivet. Then manufacture a new swing-link as shown in **Figure 5**, and attach the short end of it

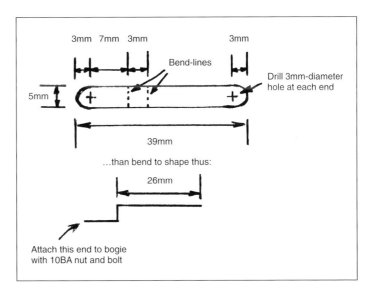

Figure 5: New bogie swing-link

to the bogie with a 10BA nut and bolt. Then attach the other end to the chassis block, and the chassis is ready for road-testing. If your chassis runs satisfactorily the ends of the 10BA screws securing the cylinder block in place can be removed with a hacksaw. Put a spot of glue on the threads of each screw, including the nut and bolt holding the bogie and its swing-link together, to prevent them working loose in traffic. With this done your chassis is now ready for painting.

Stage 2: The loco body

First remove the boiler handrails, reversing-rod and nameplates, then separate the body into its four constituent parts: cab, boiler, smokebox and running-plate. Begin the modifications by removing all six splashers from the bottom of the boiler, then, after cleaning up the sawn edges with emery cloth, fill in the resulting holes with Milliput or similar. Then remove the boiler's front extension (the part that fits inside the smokebox). Now remove the chimney, but leave the snifting-valve intact. With a craft-knife, remove the housing for the body-fixing screw from the underside of the smokebox (**Figure 6**). Using a hacksaw or craft-knife, alter the profile of the outside steam-pipes (again see **Figure 6**).

Figure 6: Modifications to smokebox

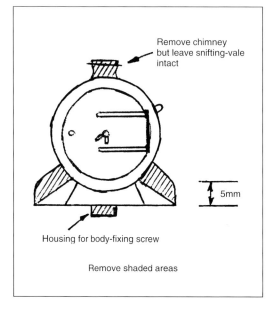

Remove chimney but leave snifting-vale intact

5mm

Housing for body-fixing screw

Remove shaded areas

Then fill in the gaps left in the tops of the steam-pipes with Milliput or similar.

In order to make the body fit the chassis we need to extend the boiler by 12mm. As luck would have it I just happened to have part of a 'D49' body in my scrap-box, and a 12mm section of its boiler fitted the bill perfectly. Alternatively, a 12mm length of 22mm-diameter broom-handle or plastic overflow pipe would be fine. Glue together the three pieces (the boiler, the new piece and the smokebox), ensuring a straight and square fit. When the glue has dried fill in any gaps with Milliput or similar. When that has set, file away any surplus with emery-cloth, and if necessary fill the gap in the vacuum-ejector pipe with a 12mm length of 1mm-diameter brass wire (suitable wire can be obtained from the Alan Gibson range).

We now turn our attention to the cab. First remove the housing for the body-fixing screw from the underside, then, using card or thin Plasticard, manufacture a pair of cab side-sheets (**Figure 7**). Glue the new side-sheets in place with their top edges butting up against the moulded horizontal handrails. When the glue has dried drill two 1mm-diameter holes through each cab side to take the handrail knobs (also **Figure 7**).

We now move on to the running-plate. First make two transverse hacksaw cuts, and retain the rear steps for further use. Then, with a craft-knife, remove all of the underside framing (**Figure 8**).

Modify the two portions of the running-plate as per **Figure 9**. The two extra 2mm-diameter holes should line-up with the two 10BA holes in the top of the R357 chassis block, which we can utilise for fixing the body and chassis block together. However, if you are using one of the other varieties of 'Patriot' chassis block, the screw-holes may be in different positions.

In order to raise the level of the running-plate above the level of the wheels, we need to manufacture a packing-piece from 1mm thick Plasticard (**Figure 10**). Glue the packing-piece to the underside of the rear portion of the running-plate (with the holes duly lined up). When the glue has set, the rear portion of the running-plate can be fixed to the chassis with two 10BA screws.

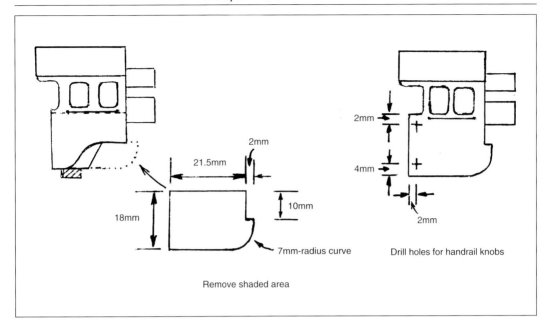

Above Figure 7: Modifications to cab

Below Figure 8: Dissection of running-plate

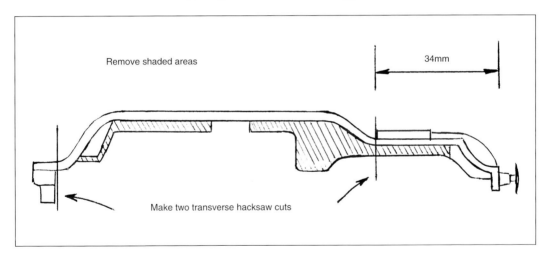

We now return to the boiler. In order to make the boiler fit over the two aforementioned 10BA screws we need to drill/cut holes in its underside to fit over the heads of the screws (**Figure 11**).

We now turn our attention to the front portion of the running-plate. First fit the lamp-brackets into the 1mm-diameter holes you drilled earlier (I used Westward lamp-brackets on my model and found them highly satisfactory). Then fit a vacuum-pipe to the front buffer-beam; for this job I used a Romford product, again highly satisfactory. With these jobs done, this portion of the running-plate can be glued to the underside of the smokebox.

At this point in the proceedings it would be a good idea to paint the boiler and apply the boiler-band transfers (in BR days all six boiler-bands were lined), then fit the boiler handrails. Next test-fit the boiler and smokebox to the chassis – you should find a noticeable gap between the top of the cylinders and the running-plate together with a 13mm gap

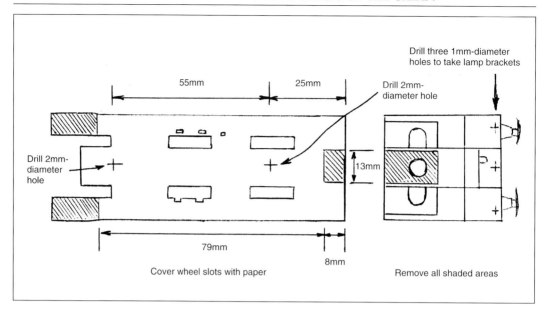

Above Figure 9: Modifications to running-plate

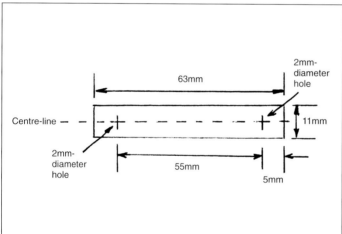

Left Figure 10: Packing-piece to raise level of running-plate

Below Figure 11: Modifications to underside of boiler

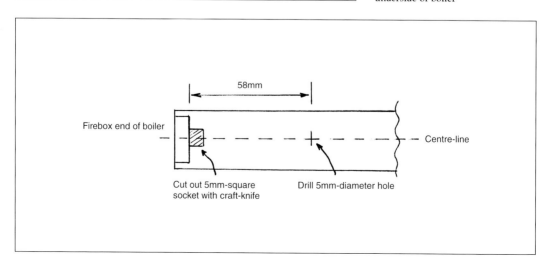

between the two sections of running-plate. So, from a sheet of 1mm-thick card or Plasticard, cut out two pieces 35mm by 11mm and glue them to the undersides of the front portion of the running-plate directly underneath the steam-pipes. These will fill the gaps between the running-plate and the cylinders, and will also provide support for the new portion of running-plate when we fit it.

Next drill a 1mm-diameter hole through the smokebox 3mm from the front, on the centre-line, to take the top lamp-bracket (I used Westward lamp-brackets on this model, which are highly satisfactory). Then fit the whistle and safety-valves – I re-used the original Hornby ones from the 'B17' – and the chimney. I used a white-metal chimney casting for a Maunsell 'King Arthur' (with capuchon), which I obtained from South Eastern Finecast – the casting is of very high quality, is very close to the required pattern, and is fitted in exactly the same position as its 'B17' predecessor. The Hornby 'B17' dome is of the correct pattern and is in the correct position for a rebuilt 'B16', so requires no modification.

With this work done, the boiler can be glued to the rear portion of the running-plate. When the glue has dried we can turn our attention to the gaps between the two portions of running-plate. First, from a sheet of 80 thou (2mm)-thick Plasticard, cut out two pieces 13mm by 11mm, file to fit if necessary and glue them in place to bridge the gap between the two sections of running-plate.

We now need to fabricate the portions of running-plate that follow the undersides of the cab, including the 7mm-radius quadrant. I found a product ideal for this task in 60 thou x 40 thou (1.5mm by 1mm) plastic strip produced by Evergreen Plastics (an American firm whose products are stocked by many model shops, including Mainly Trains, who also do mail-order). The 60 thou size is ideal for representing the running-plate, and it can be bent to the required profile between the thumb and forefinger. After bending and cutting to the required length, glue the new sections of running-plate in place, holding them in position with a bulldog clip or sprung clothes-peg until the glue has dried.

With the under-cab sections of the running-plate securely in position, we can think about the cab steps, and we shall need something to fix them to. Evergreen Plastics also produce packs of 100 thou (2.5mm) square plastic strip. Cut two 13mm lengths and glue them to the inside edge of each cab side-sheet with their bottom and rear edges in line with those of the cab side-sheets. When the adhesive has dried, glue the cab steps in place with their rear edges in line with the rear of the cab; on my model I re-used the plastic steps from the 'B17'.

Next, *if building one of the Thompson locos*, we need to fit a pair of rear sandboxes to the underside of the cab, between the steps and the rear driving wheels (on the Gresley locos the rear sandboxes were out of sight inside the cab). A pair of white-metal castings suitable for this job is available from Jackson-Evans (item No W.95 in their range – 'G.W. County Sandboxes'). The castings are of very good quality and come with small holes drilled in the bottom to take a piece of wire (to represent the sand delivery pipe). On my model I used two 10mm lengths of 0.7mm-diameter brass wire (obtainable from Alan Gibson) and bent it to shape as per **Figure 12**. With this done I glued each length of wire into the small holes in the base of each casting, then glued each assembly to the undersides of the cab immediately adjacent to the cab steps.

Figure 12: Rear sand-boxes

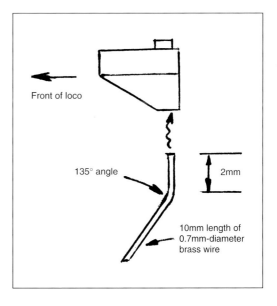

Front of loco

135° angle

2mm

10mm length of 0.7mm-diameter brass wire

With the rear sandboxes in place we can fit the cab section to the rest of the loco. Note the square holes in the cab front (to clear the 27mm-diameter wheels of the 'B17'), and the holes in the side of the firebox caused by the removal of the rear splashers. Fill these holes with Milliput or similar, or cover them with paper.

We can now move on to the oil-boxes situated on top of the 'S' curves of the running-plate. First cut out two pieces of 5mm by 2mm 80 thou (2mm)-thick Plasticard and glue one to each running-plate in line with the rear of the second boiler-band (**Figure 13**). Next cut out two further pieces of 10mm by 5mm 80 thou Plasticard and glue them in place with their leading edges resting on top of the previously mentioned 5mm by 2mm pieces (**Figure 13** again). Then fill in the triangular gaps with Milliput or similar. With this done, the leading sand-fillers can be glued in place. On my model I used a pair of white-metal castings from Craftsman Models (item No 95 in their range) (again see **Figure 13**). Then fit the Wakefield mechanical lubricators – both the Gresley and the Thompson locos had two on the left-hand side. White-metal castings are available from many sources, including South Eastern Finecast,

Craftsman Models and Dave Alexander; the last-mentioned are particularly good, having a separately cast brass wheel.

Next, from a piece of 2mm-wide brass strip or plastic microstrip, manufacture a reversing-rod. This needs to be 85mm long, and for a Thompson rebuild it needs to go on the left-hand side (for a Gresley loco it would need to go on the right-hand side). On both variations the reversing-rod enters the cab 5mm above the level of the running-plate, while its leading end disappears out of sight behind the oil-box (see again **Figure 13**). With this job done we can move on to the tender.

Stage 3: The tender

All of the 'B16s' ran with North Eastern 4,125-gallon 'self-trimming' tenders with short coal-rails that were curved both front and rear (as fitted to the North Eastern 'Atlantics' and some 'Q6s'). Dave Alexander produces a white-metal kit, while DMR Products Ltd produces an etched-brass kit, which would require some proficiency in soldering in order to construct it. However, both tender bodies would still need modification to fit the Hornby 'B17'/'D49'

Figure 13: Running-plate oil-boxes, etc

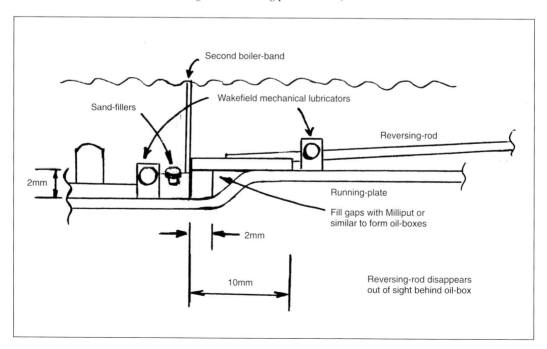

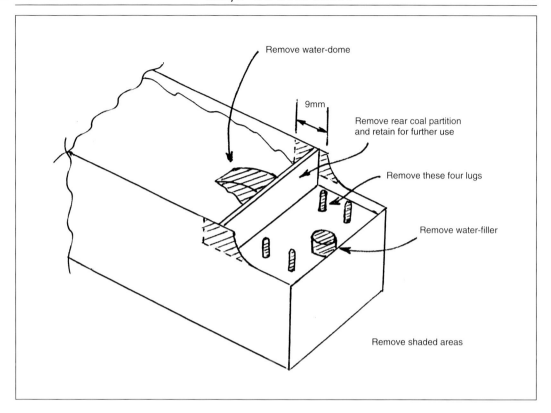

Remove water-dome

9mm

Remove rear coal partition
and retain for further use

Remove these four lugs

Remove water-filler

Remove shaded areas

Above Figure 14: Modifications to
Hornby 'B17' tender

Above right and right The completed
tender.

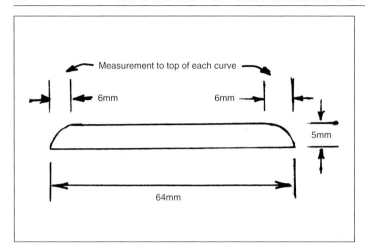

Figure 15: New tender side-raves

tender chassis and power unit. I preferred to modify the Hornby 'B17'/'D49' tender body, putting the difference in length (6mm) down to 'modeller's licence'. The method of construction is as follows.

First dismantle the rear of the tender (**Figure 14**), and replace the rear coal partition 5mm forward of its original position. The removal of the LNER-pattern water-dome will have left a square hole in the top of the coal space; cover this with a piece of paper glued to the underside, and cover the upper side of the paper with imitation coal. Next fit an NER-pattern water-filler in the same position as its 'B17' predecessor and a round water-dome in the gap between the water-filler and the rear coal partition. Suitable white-metal castings for both the water-filler and water-dome are available from Dave Alexander, DMR Products Ltd and Dave Bradwell (from his 'B1' tender kit). On my model I used the Dave Alexander products.

Next manufacture a new pair of side-raves from 1mm-thick card or Plasticard (**Figure 15**), and glue them to the tender body with their top edges level with the top edges of the tender body. Glue strips of 1mm square microstrip to the outside edges of the water space, to give it the appearance of a flared top. Then manufacture the coal-rails from 1mm-diameter brass wire (available from Alan Gibson), with the top rail on each side following the contours of the side-raves (use photographs as a guide).

With this job completed your model is ready for painting and transfers. The livery carried in BR days was 'mixed traffic', and the route availability number was RA8.

This loco was the most complicated conversion I had ever carried out at the time, but was well worth it, as I think the photographs show! The model negotiates second-radius curves and small-radius pointwork without any difficulty.

Ex-LNER 'D20/2' 4-4-0 No 62349

In 1899 the North Eastern Railway introduced its Class 'R' 4-4-0 locomotives. They were very successful and proved very popular with their crews. Sixty were built and they all survived to become LNER Class 'D20' at the Grouping in 1923. In 1936 Gresley decided to rebuild one with long-travel piston-valves (10 inches instead of 8¾ inches). While it was Gresley's idea, it fell to Edward Thompson, who was Mechanical Engineer (North Eastern Area) based at Darlington, to supervise (and take responsibility for) the rebuilding. During the process Thompson took the opportunity to remove the large North Eastern-pattern splashers and raise the running-plate over the driving wheels (to achieve greater 'getatability'). The result was something that vaguely resembled an LMS '2P'. The loco chosen for rebuilding was LNER No 2020, which happened to be in Darlington Works for general overhaul at the time.

When Gresley saw the rebuilt loco for the first time on a visit to Darlington Works late in 1936 he gave Thompson a dressing-down on the shop-floor in front of all of his (Thompson's) subordinates. Thompson never forgave Gresley for this and their relations were suitably soured and strained until Gresley's death in 1941. Only three further engines were rebuilt (the outward appearance of these locos was not altered), so any improvement in performance must have been minimal.

In 1948 LNER No 2020 became British Railways property as No 62349. It had an unspectacular life, although (together with the other members of the class) it established a reputation for reliability and hard work. It spent time allocated to Alnmouth, Heaton, Blaydon, York, Starbeck and Selby, and was finally withdrawn off Selby (50C) in February 1956. So we have another unusual loco that ran for almost 20 years in its rebuilt form, and a useful addition to any North Eastern layout.

Items required

Hornby/Dapol/Mainline ex-LMS '2P' 4-4-0 loco; Hornby Class 'B17' loco cab; Class 'B17' reversing-rod; detailing parts as described in text.

Stage 1: The '2P' loco body

First of all separate the '2P' loco body from the chassis; they are held together by a screw underneath the cab and a brass screw at the front end, which also holds the bogie in place. Next remove the LMS-style pipework from the left-hand side of the smokebox. Remove the cab, which is a separate moulding glued in place; gentle coaxing with a penknife blade should remove it. With the cab gone it is now possible to remove the smokebox door – a gentle push from behind with a pen or pencil should do the trick!

Next remove the whistle and safety-valves and retain them for re-use. With a hacksaw or craft-knife, remove the chimney and dome, and fill in the resultant holes with Milliput or similar. Next remove the front steps and file flush any residue. As we will be doing a bit of work on the loco's front end later (lamp-brackets, 'piano-front' and new smokebox door) it may be an idea to remove the front vacuum-pipe to avoid damaging it.

As all the 'D20s' (including No 62349) had continuous boiler handrails, we shall have to remove the handrails of the '2P' (leave the knobs in place, however – we can re-employ

Above 'D20/2' 4-4-0 No 62349, still with 'LNER' on its tender when photographed at Heaton shed on 25 June 1950. *W. G. Boyden, courtesy of Frank Hornby*

Below The completed model.

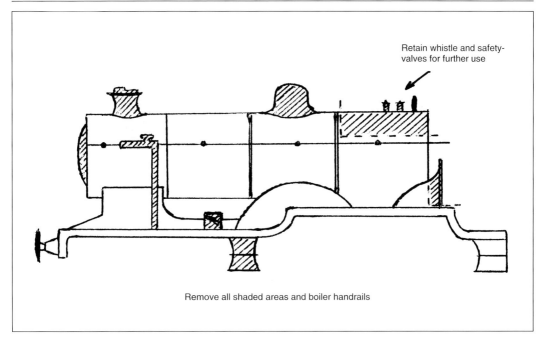

Retain whistle and safety-valves for further use

Remove all shaded areas and boiler handrails

Figure 1: '2P' loco body after removal of cab

them on the new model); a penknife blade and a pair of pliers should do the trick! Next remove both mechanical lubricators with a craft-knife, then remove the top of the Belpaire firebox with two horizontal saw cuts just above the two handrail knobs on each side of the firebox, and a vertical saw cut as near as possible to the front of the firebox without damaging the adjacent boiler-band. Then clean up the edges of the cuts with a file or emery-cloth (**Figure 1**). With the removal of the cab it will be noticed that the rear ends of the rear splashers protrude further back than the rear of the firebox; cut these back so that the rear of the splashers is in line with the rear of the firebox (again see **Figure 1**). Then, from card or Plasticard, manufacture a pair of outside panels for the rear splashers.

We now move on to the most 'fiddly' part of this conversion – the re-profiling of the leading splashers. The outside panels of the splashers are separate mouldings glued in place and are easily removed with a bit of pressure from the inside. Having removed the splashers, with a craft-knife cut away an area 5mm by 2mm from their bottom edges (**Figure 2**). Then dissect each side of the running-plate adjacent to the leading

quadrants (also **Figure 2**) and file down the resulting two severed pieces of running-plate to a width of 2mm so that they will fit onto the outside edges of the outer panels of each splasher (**Figure 3**). Glue the outer panels of each splasher back into their original positions, then re-assemble the leading quadrants (also **Figure 3**).

From card manufacture a new (round) top for the firebox, 26mm square (**Figure 4**). Drill three 1mm-diameter holes (on the centre-line) at 4mm intervals to take the whistle and safety-valves. Bend the new firebox top to shape and glue in place (trimming if necessary), then cover the firebox with a piece of paper to hide the joins and the 'threepenny-bit effect' (**Figure 5**).

Next, from card or Plasticard manufacture a new pair of frames for the front end (**Figure 6**), then glue in place (the rear end of each frame should butt up to the edge of the leading splasher, while the leading end should be in line with the top edge of the buffer-beam – use photographs as a guide). Cut out a rectangular piece of card or Plasticard 17mm by 8mm (to form the 'piano-front') and glue in place between the frames in front of the smokebox, thus covering the piston tail-rods of the '2P'.

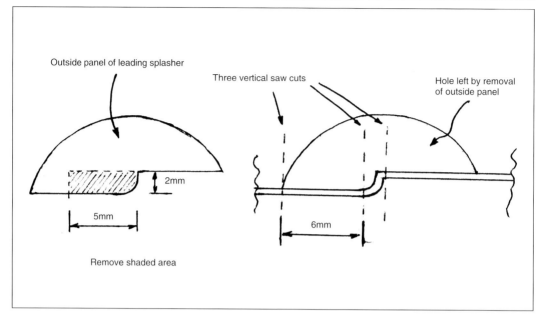

Outside panel of leading splasher

Three vertical saw cuts

Hole left by removal of outside panel

2mm

5mm

Remove shaded area

6mm

Above Figure 2: Modifications to leading splashers and running-plate

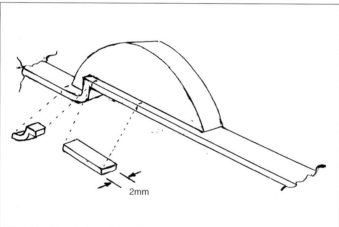

2mm

Left Figure 3: Reassembly of leading quadrants

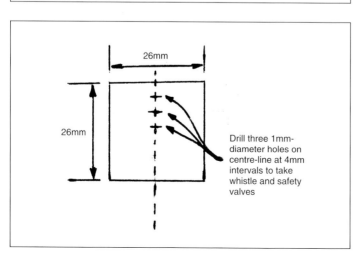

26mm

26mm

Drill three 1mm-diameter holes on centre-line at 4mm intervals to take whistle and safety valves

Left Figure 4: New top for firebox

Figure 5: Paper cover for top of firebox

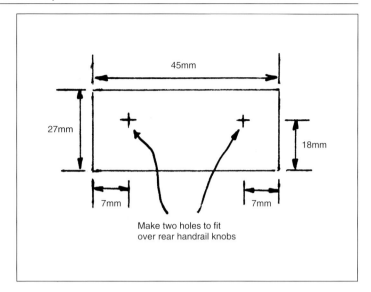

Right Figure 6: Making frames for front end

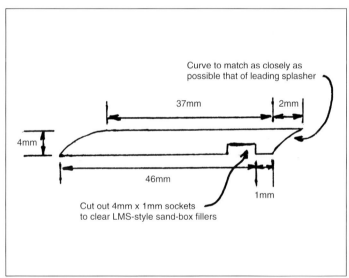

Below Figure 7: Making new smokebox front

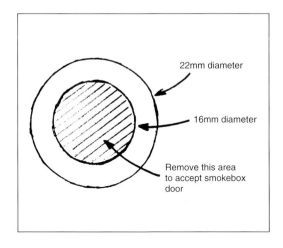

We now move on to the smokebox door. No 62349 had a door noticeably smaller in diameter than the outside rim of the smokebox. For my model I used a 'J21' smokebox door from Dave Alexander; at 16mm diameter it is about right for our loco and it comes ready drilled to take a Markits (or similar) handle. In order to fit it to the loco I manufactured a new front for the smokebox from card (**Figure 7**), then glued it in place.

Drill three 1mm-diameter holes through the running-plate immediately above the buffer-beam to take the lamp-brackets. These go in the usual places: one above the front coupling and the other two above each buffer 3mm in from each outside edge of the running-plate. Then drill another 1mm-diameter hole through the top of the smokebox on the centre-line, 1mm from its leading edge, to take the top lamp-bracket. While you have the drill in your hand, drill another 1mm-diameter hole 3mm from the rear edge of the smokebox, on the centre-line, to take the snifting-valve.

Stage 2: The 'B17' cab

First, with a hacksaw or craft-knife, remove the front protrusions (intended to fit inside the 'B17' boiler) and file any residue flush. Next, with the hacksaw, remove the socket for the body-fixing screw, then remove the cab floor, the seats, and the firehole door (to clear the driving wheels of the '2P'). Remove 3mm from the bottom of the cab side-sheets (**Figure 8**). Test-fit the 'B17' cab to the '2P' chassis and you should find a small gap on each side of the loco between the bottom of the cab and the rear quadrants, two gaps adjacent to the rear splashers (the 'B17' splashers were wider than those of the '2P'), and a small gap just above the top of the firebox (the 'B17' boiler was higher pitched than that of the '2P'). The last-mentioned problem can be solved by either filling in the hole in the front of the cab with

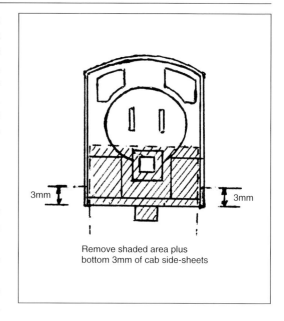

Remove shaded area plus
bottom 3mm of cab side-sheets

Figure 8: Rear view of 'B17' cab

Milliput or similar, or covering it over with paper. Likewise the gaps adjacent to the quadrants and splashers can be covered over with paper (**Figure 9**). With these jobs done, the cab can be glued in place. However, more enterprising modellers may wish to manufacture a new pair of cab seats and cab floor from card or similar before finally gluing the cab in place.

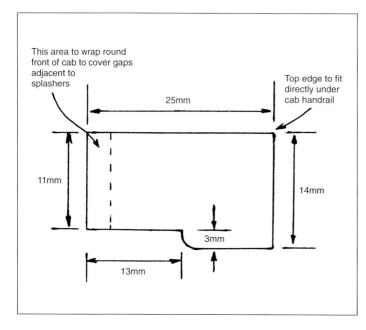

This area to wrap round
front of cab to cover gaps
adjacent to
splashers

Top edge to fit
directly under
cab handrail

25mm

11mm

14mm

3mm

13mm

Figure 9: Manufacture of paper covers for cab side-sheets

Stage 3: Finishing the loco body

When LNER No 2020 (62349) was rebuilt in 1936 it was changed to left-hand drive, as were the other three rebuilt locos (LNER Class 'D20/2'). So we need to fit a vacuum-ejector (regulator) pipe along the left-hand side of the boiler 3mm above the handrail, running from the cab to the midway point of the smokebox (76mm). Use a length of 1mm-diameter handrail wire or one of Hornby's plastic mouldings (intended for use on their 'A3'), which at the time of writing are still available from Modelspares and East Kent Models. Likewise the reversing-rod goes on the left-hand side. I used a Hornby 'B17' reversing-rod with the round screw-hole removed and glued it along the side of the boiler with its curved end following the curve of the leading splasher (use photographs as a guide). Next we need to fit a Wakefield mechanical lubricator to the right-hand running-plate 34mm from the front edge of the buffer-beam. Castings for these are available from many manufacturers; Dave Alexander produces some particularly good ones that have a separate brass wheel.

Next glue the whistle and safety-valves of the '2P' into the holes you drilled in the top of the firebox, and fit the lamp-brackets – Westward produce some particularly good ones. Glue the snifting-valve into the hole that you drilled through the top of the smokebox – again, castings for these are available from many sources (I used one from DMR Products Ltd). As regards the chimney, I used a white-metal casting supplied by the proprietor of Little Engines (from his 'A7' kit). The centre of the chimney needs to be 9mm from the leading edge of the smokebox.

No 62349 carried two different types of dome during its lifetime. For most of its life it carried a tall narrow affair as fitted to the 'A7s' (again use a casting from Little Engines). However, some time in the 1940s the loco was fitted with a 'shorter and fatter' dome, the dimensions of which are almost identical to the LB&SCR Class 'E2'; sources are South Eastern Finecast, or even Hornby (their 'E2' has been out of production for some time now, but the body moulding lives on as 'Thomas the Tank Engine'!). The centre of both types of dome needs to be fitted 44mm from the leading edge of the smokebox.

Next return the vacuum brake-pipe of the '2P' to its original position on the buffer-beam. Fit the boiler handrail utilising the original '2P' handrail-knobs; all of the 'D20s' had continuous handrails that curved around the top of the smokebox door (use photographs as a guide). The handrails on my model are manufactured from a 210mm length of 0.45mm-diameter brass wire supplied by Alan Gibson.

We now turn our attention to the front steps. The 'D20s' (in common with other North Eastern classes) had very elaborate front steps (see photographs). Possible sources of suitable castings are Little Engines (from their 'A6' kit) and Autocomm Ltd (from their 'Nu-Cast' 'F4' kit). However, if you are unable to obtain these castings you could manufacture your own from card (**Figure 10**). Glue them to the underside of each running-plate 36mm to the rear of the buffer-beam, ensure that the steps do not interfere with the swing of the bogie. With this job done, the loco body is complete.

Figure 10: Manufacture of new front steps

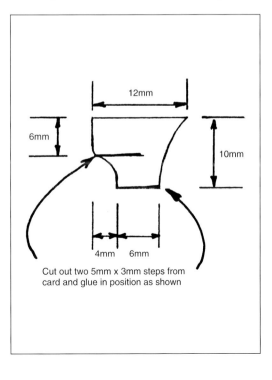

Cut out two 5mm x 3mm steps from card and glue in position as shown

Stage 4: The tender

When Edward Thompson completed his rebuilding of LNER No 2020 the standard North Eastern 4,125-gallon tender was transformed into something that resembled the Great Western 'Collett Intermediate' tender as coupled to some '2251s', some '73xxs', and some 'Manors' (consult photographs). You could therefore utilise a tender body from the Mainline or Bachmann '2251', but it would require a lot of modification. It would need to be shortened and the top of the tender would need to be completely removed to clear the power unit of the '2P' (and then camouflaged); also the Bachmann model has riveted sides, whereas No 2020's tender was smooth-sided. I consider that modifying the '2P' tender would be a better option.

First, with the craft-knife, remove the beading from the top edge of the rear of the tender. Then, with a hacksaw, remove 3.5mm from the top of the sides (**Figure 11**). Next drill out the water-filler, then, with the craft-knife, remove the tender vents. Fill in or cover over the hole left by the removal of the water-filler and fit an LNER-pattern water-filler (very good castings for these are available from Craftsman Models, South Eastern Finecast and Dave Alexander). Fit a pair of tender vents 5mm behind the front coal partition; LMS-pattern tender vents are available from Westward and Jackson-Evans and are very close to the required profile.

Figuring out how to manufacture the stepped-out coping took a while until I hit on the idea of making spacers for the rear and sides from 2.5mm square microstrip (**Figure 12**). Glue the spacers to the sides and rear of the tender body (**Figure 13**). Next, manufacture the tender coping from *paper* (**Figure 14**); cut out two pieces of paper,

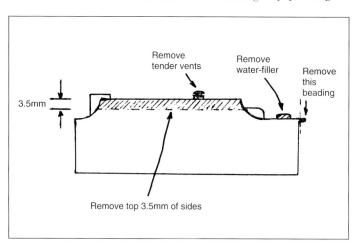

Figure 11: Dissection of tender body

Remove tender vents

Remove water-filler

Remove this beading

3.5mm

Remove top 3.5mm of sides

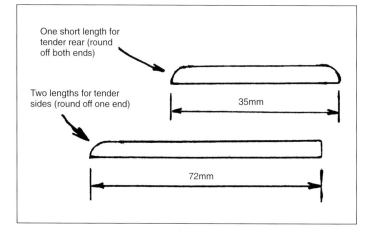

One short length for tender rear (round off both ends)

Two lengths for tender sides (round off one end)

35mm

72mm

Figure 12: Spacers for stepped-out coping

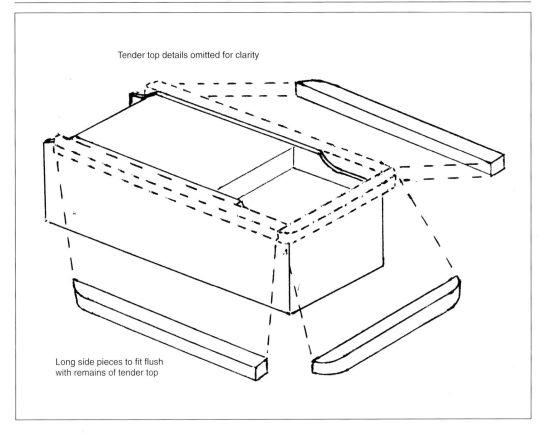

Tender top details omitted for clarity

Long side pieces to fit flush
with remains of tender top

Above Figure 13: Fitting spacers for stepped-out coping

Below Figure 14: Manufacture of new tender coping

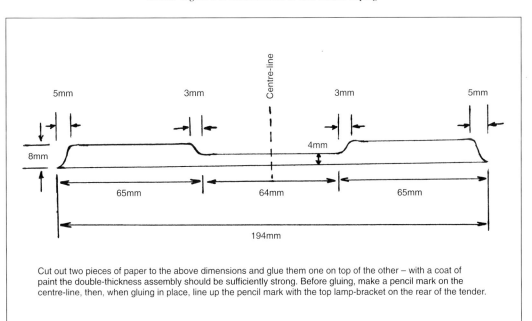

Centre-line

5mm   3mm   3mm   5mm

8mm

4mm

65mm   64mm   65mm

194mm

Cut out two pieces of paper to the above dimensions and glue them one on top of the other – with a coat of
paint the double-thickness assembly should be sufficiently strong. Before gluing, make a pencil mark on the
centre-line, then, when gluing in place, line up the pencil mark with the top lamp-bracket on the rear of the tender.

Left and below left The modified tender body, showing the new 'stepped-out' coping.

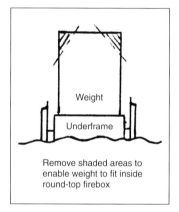

Below Figure 15: Modifications to chassis weight

Weight

Underframe

Remove shaded areas to enable weight to fit inside round-top firebox

glue them one on top of the other, then glue them to the coping spacers with the centre-line pencil-mark lined up with the top lamp-bracket on the rear of the tender.

From card or Plasticard manufacture new partitions for the coal space, 36mm by 4mm, and glue them to the original partitions. We now have a gap between the top of the coping and the coal, so fill this with Milliput or similar and cover with imitation coal. As regards the bracket for the fire-irons, No 62349 did have something on top of the tender to hold them, but not having seen any overhead views of the loco I don't know what form this bracket took – so leave the LMS bracket in situ. The tender is now complete.

Stage 5: The loco chassis

Only one small modification needs to be made to the loco chassis: the large weight over the driving wheels is designed to fit inside a Belpaire firebox (completely filling the space inside). Because we are changing the firebox to the round-topped variety we need to file a few millimetres off the top edges of the weight (**Figure 15**). When the completed body fits comfortably over the weight the chassis is complete.

The loco is now ready for painting and transfers. The livery carried in BR days was unlined black, and the route availability was RA6. The only BR emblem that this loco carried was the 'lion and unicycle'. So there we have it – another useful and unusual addition to any ex-North Eastern layout.

Ex-LNER 'Q6' 0-8-0 No 63417

In 1913 the North Eastern Railway introduced its class 'T2' 0-8-0 freight locomotives, which were designed by Sir Vincent Raven. The design employed a 5ft 6in-diameter boiler, two cylinders, and 4ft 7¼in-diameter wheels. A total of 120 examples were built and they all survived to become LNER Class 'Q6' in 1923. Like the 'Q5s', these locos had steam-reversers, but they were hidden away out of sight behind the rear sandbox. During the 1930s the LNER began replacing the original NER-pattern domes with a flatter, squarer dome (identical to that of the 'B17'), and eventually the whole class were so fitted.

All 120 locos survived to become BR property in 1948. Although the 'Q6s' were only ever allocated to North Eastern sheds, after the Grouping they could be seen regularly in Scotland (one was even recorded as reaching Aberdeen). The most southerly North Eastern sheds (York, Neville Hill, Selby, Dairycoates and Normanton) all had 'Q6s' allocated to them, and they regularly worked south of the North Eastern frontier onto the Eastern Region. In addition, the Dairycoates locos worked regularly to Manchester (Mottram Yard) via Woodhead until that route was electrified. Also Dairycoates locos visiting Doncaster were often purloined by Doncaster Control for its own duties and there are records of Dairycoates 'Q6s' reaching Immingham (on the south side of the river), New England and even Ferme Park in London.

The 'Q6s' built up a reputation for hard work and reliability and were one of the most popular classes of loco ever to run on rails! I've never met anyone with a bad word to say about them. Withdrawals began with No 63372 in May 1960 – when you think about it, that is outstanding for a pre-Grouping design. The final withdrawals

came in September 1967 with the withdrawal of No 63395 off Sunderland, together with Nos 63344 and 63387 off West Hartlepool. No 63395 was later purchased for preservation. Here, then, is another long-lived class (54 years' service), with examples seen on many parts of the LNER system – another useful addition to any ex-LNER layout.

Items required

Hornby (Margate) '28xx' loco chassis and loco body; Hornby 'B17' loco body; Hornby 'B17'/'D49' complete tender (including power unit)

Stage 1: The '28xx' loco body

For our new model we only require the running-plate and splashers of the '28xx', so we have to indulge in some extreme vandalism on the loco body. First make a horizontal hacksaw cut through the cab and firebox at floor level, then cut through the two pipes leading from the top-feed to the running-plate. Next make another horizontal saw cut through the base of the smokebox saddle at running-plate level. Cut through the boiler support brackets abaft the leading splashers and clean up any rough edges with a file or emery-cloth (**Figure 1**). Next, with a craft-knife, remove the GWR-style bracket on the underside of the right-hand running-plate, and both mechanical lubricators from each running-plate.

We next need to remove the GWR-pattern cab steps, the rear frame-mounted sandboxes, and the rear 6mm of the footplate. First make two horizontal saw cuts through the tops of the cab steps, immediately below the footplate, then

Above The locomotive being modelled, 'Q6' 0-8-0 No 63417, was photographed at Cardigan Road goods, Leeds, on 3 April 1964. *David Holmes*

Below The completed loco, a good-looking model and based on a British-made '28xx' chassis!

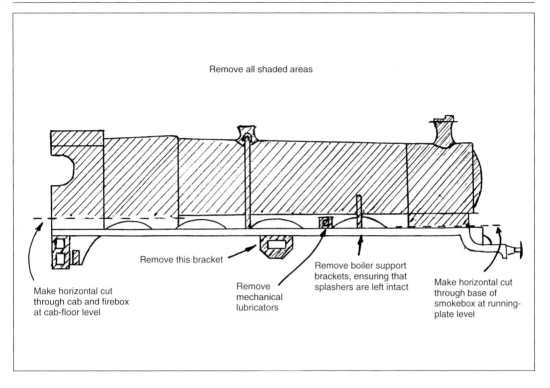

Remove all shaded areas

Remove this bracket

Remove mechanical lubricators

Remove boiler support brackets, ensuring that splashers are left intact

Make horizontal cut through cab and firebox at cab-floor level

Make horizontal cut through base of smokebox at running-plate level

Figure 1: Dissection of '28xx' body

Figure 2: Removal of cab steps and rear sand-boxes

Figure 3: Removal of rear 6mm of footplate

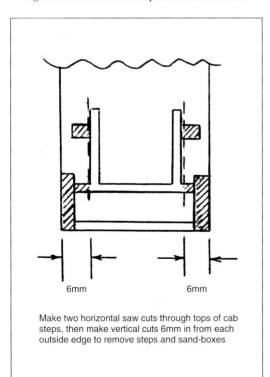

6mm   6mm

Make two horizontal saw cuts through tops of cab steps, then make vertical cuts 6mm in from each outside edge to remove steps and sand-boxes

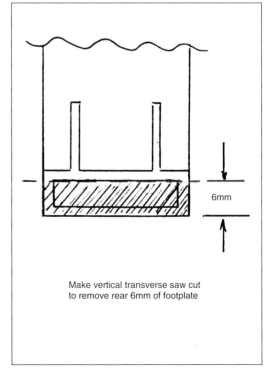

6mm

Make vertical transverse saw cut to remove rear 6mm of footplate

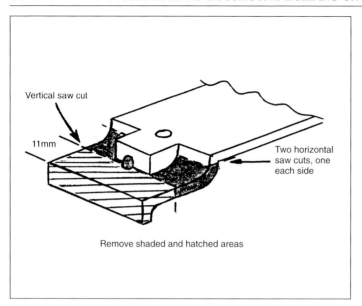

Left Figure 4: Dissection of '28xx' front end

Below Figure 5: Further dissection of '28xx' front end

make two vertical saw cuts 6mm from the outside edges of the footplate (**Figure 2**); this should take care of the steps and sandboxes. Next make a vertical transverse saw cut to remove the rear 6mm of the footplate (**Figure 3**).

We now turn our attention to the front end of the running-plate, with a vertical transverse saw cut immediately in front of the 'piano-front', removing the buffer-beam and the front 11mm of the running-plate (**Figure 4**). Then remove the remains of the quadrants on either side of the 'piano-front' with two horizontal saw cuts in line with the bottom edges of the running-plate, and two vertical cuts in line with the outside edges of the 'piano-front' (also **Figure 4**). Finally clean up the sawn edges with a file or emery-cloth.

We now, somehow, need to construct a new buffer-beam for our model, and I used the following method. First, from the portion of the running-plate that we removed earlier (in **Figure 4**), cut out two rectangular pieces 9mm by 3mm and glue them to the front of the running-plate and the sides of the 'piano-front' (**Figure 5**). Then manufacture a new buffer-beam from 1mm-thick Plasticard 34.5mm by 9mm, and drill three 2mm-diameter holes (**Figure 6**) to take the buffers and coupling-hook. Next glue three lamp-brackets to its inner face (I used the Westward variety on my model) and glue the buffer-beam to the front of the running-plate. When the glue has set, glue a piece of paper

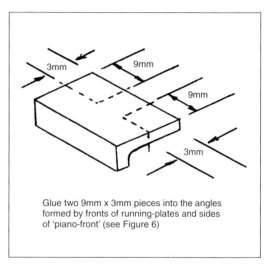

Glue two 9mm x 3mm pieces into the angles formed by fronts of running-plates and sides of 'piano-front' (see Figure 6)

34mm by 11mm over the newly assembled front portion of the running-plate to cover over and reinforce the joins. Finally, cut or file away 2mm from each side of the cab floor to allow the fitting of the 'B17' cab.

Stage 2: The 'B17' loco-body

First of all remove the protrusions from the front of the cab (used for holding the boiler in place), then cover over or fill in the resulting hole (**Figure 8**). Next remove the screw-socket housing from the underside of the cab, then remove the bottom 6mm from the inside of the

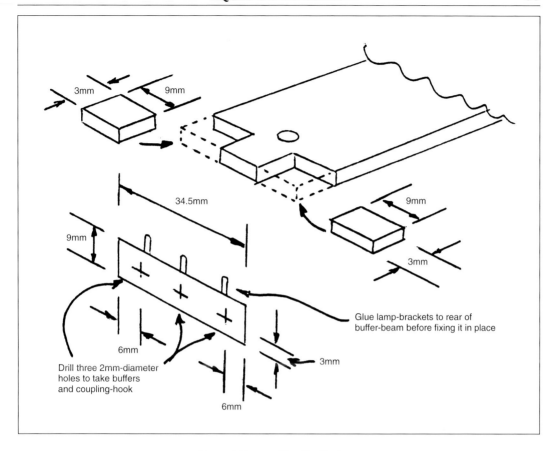

3mm   9mm

34.5mm   9mm

9mm   3mm

Glue lamp-brackets to rear of
buffer-beam before fixing it in place

6mm   3mm

Drill three 2mm-diameter
holes to take buffers
and coupling-hook

6mm

Figure 6: Reassembly of buffer-beam

cab (to enable it to fit over the '28xx' cab floor). *Leave the cab side-sheets intact* (**Figure 7**). Next remove 2mm from the bottom of the cab side-sheets (again see **Figure 8**). Clean up the sawn edges with a file or emery-cloth and offer the cab to the '28xx' running-plate. If it is a straight and square fit, move on to the boiler.

The 'B17' boiler needs to be shortened by 6mm, and this is best achieved by making two vertical saw cuts (6mm apart) between the third and fourth boiler-bands (**Figure 9**). After cleaning up the sawn edges remove the vacuum-ejector pipe and the splashers with a craft-knife. Then glue the two parts of the boiler together; when the glue has set, use Milliput or similar to fill in any remaining gaps including the holes left by the removal of the splashers.

As regards the smokebox, seven items need to be removed: the screw-socket housing on the underside of the saddle, the chimney, the vacuum-ejector pipe, the two superheater

headers, and the two outside steam-pipes. Then cut or file down the outside edges of the smokebox saddle to a vertical profile (**Figures 10 and 11**), and clean up any rough edges with a file or emery-cloth. Finally, the removal of the outside steam-pipes will have left a couple of holes in the side of the smokebox; fill these with Milliput or similar. The boiler and smokebox can now be fitted together in readiness for re-assembly.

Stage 3: Reassembling the loco-body

First manufacture new cab side-sheets from paper (**Figure 12**) and glue in place, wrapped around the front and sides of the 'B17' cab, then glue the cab in place at the rear of the '28xx' running-plate. Cut out a piece of card (**Figure 13**) and glue to the stump of the '28xx' firebox. Then test-fit the boiler and smokebox onto the

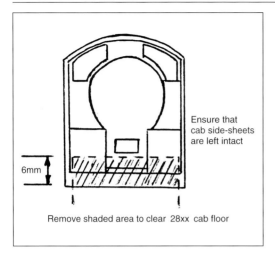

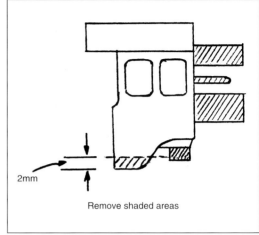

Figure 7: Rear view of 'B17' cab   Figure 8: Side view of 'B17' cab

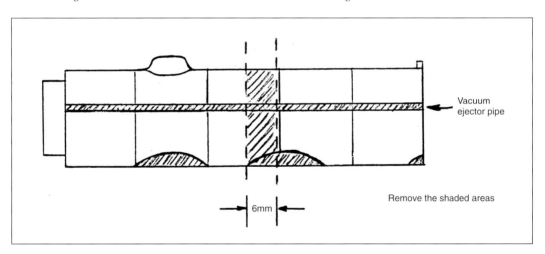

Figure 9: The 'B17' boiler

Figure 10: The 'B17' smokebox   Figure 11: Front view of smokebox

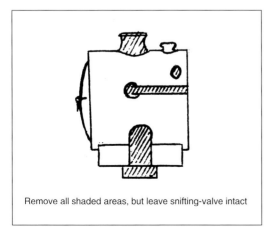

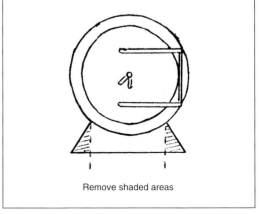

Figure 12: Manufacture of new cab sides

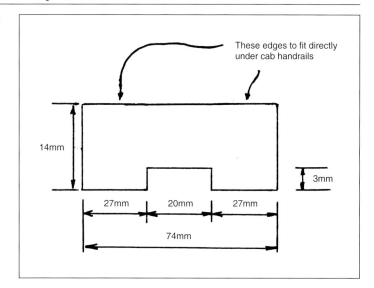

These edges to fit directly under cab handrails

14mm

3mm

27mm   20mm   27mm

74mm

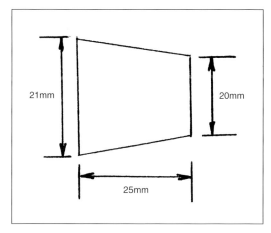

21mm

20mm

25mm

Figure 13: New base for firebox

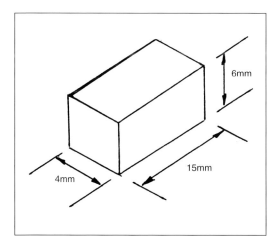

8mm to top of curve

5mm

27mm

Figure 14: Front frame extensions

Figure 15: Manufacture of rear sand-boxes

Figure 16: New combined front splashers and sand-boxes

6mm

15mm

4mm

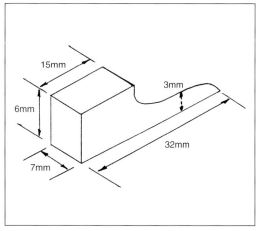

15mm

3mm

6mm

32mm

7mm

'28xx' running-plate; if they sit straight and level, glue them in place. Next cut out two pieces of thin card or paper 45mm by 2mm, and glue them to the inside edges of the first, second and third splashers (thus forming the rear frames). From two pieces of card, manufacture the front frame extensions (**Figure 14**) and glue them to the outside edges of the smokebox saddle with their leading edges in line with the buffer-beam (use photographs as a guide).

Next, from card or Plasticard, manufacture the large rear sandboxes (**Figure 15**), and glue them in place directly over the third splasher on each side of the loco. Then, from card, manufacture the combined front splashers and sandboxes (**Figure 16**), and glue them in place over the original splashers. Fit a Wakefield mechanical lubricator to the right-hand running-plate; originally, this item was situated immediately to the rear of the leading splasher, up against the frames, but in BR days it was moved to sit immediately in advance of the rear sandbox, on the outside edge of the running-plate. Castings for mechanical lubricators are available from many manufacturers, including Dave Alexander, who produces some particularly good ones incorporating a separate brass wheel.

The next task is the fitting of the cab steps. The nearest I could find to the correct North Eastern pattern were from Jackson-Evans (item M.294 'LMS Stanier tender footsteps' in their catalogue). That done, move on to the fitting of the boiler handrail. I used Alan Gibson 'medium'-size handrail knobs stuck into the original holes in the 'B17' boiler, combined with Alan Gibson 0.45mm-diameter brass wire. This was probably the hardest job of the whole conversion, but the end result was well worth the effort.

We now turn our attention to the boiler-mountings. First drill a 1mm-diameter hole through the top of the smokebox 3mm from its leading edge, on the centre-line, and insert the top lamp-bracket (I used the Westward variety). Next fit the safety-valves and whistle (I re-used the ones from the 'B17'). As regards the dome, I retained the original 'B17' version, which is satisfactory for the 'Q6' in its later years. If your model is pre-1930, however, you will need an 'Early Q6 dome' available from Dave Alexander. This earlier-pattern dome would go in the same

position as its 'B17' predecessor. A very good white-metal casting for the chimney is available from Dave Alexander (from his 'Q6' kit), and this would need to be fitted in the same position as the 'B17' chimney. Be careful when selecting an identity for your model, however, for there were four 'Q6s' that I know of that had the capuchons removed from their chimneys (for working on the Waverley route north of Carlisle); these were Nos 63373, 63414, 63416 and 63431.

Next fit a coupling-hook to the centre of the buffer-beam together with the buffers. On my model I used Cavendish sprung buffers (item No 9 in their range 'LNER/SR stepped parallel'), and very good they are too!

Stage 4: The loco chassis

Apart from the removal of the pony-truck the only work required on the loco chassis is the fabrication of a front coupling. To achieve this I threaded a 6BA bolt through the holes in the running-plate and the top of the chassis (this also serves to hold the body and chassis together). I then threaded onto the bolt a 5mm-thick piece of balsa-wood 13mm by 10mm (**Figure 17**). I cut a piece of 0.5mm-thick brass to the same dimensions as the balsa-wood (**Figure 18**), then took a 44mm length of 1mm-diameter brass wire, bent it to shape and soldered it to the brass plate (also **Figure 18**). I finally threaded everything onto the 6BA bolt (**Figure 19**).

Figure 17: Fabrication of coupling-block

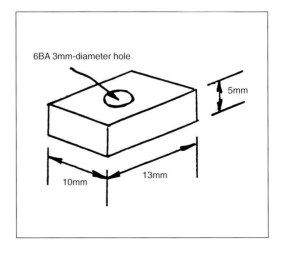

6BA 3mm-diameter hole

5mm

10mm

13mm

Figure 18: New front coupling

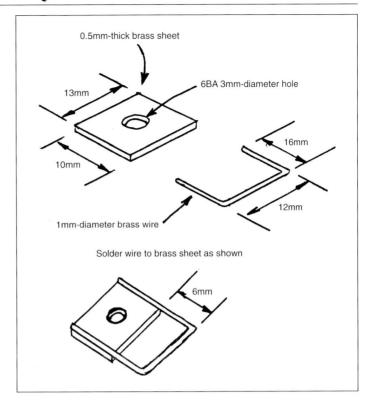

Figure 19: Assembly of front coupling

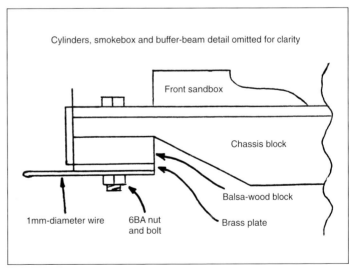

Stage 5: The tender

The 'Q6s' were quipped with six types of tender:

1 3,940 gallons with four coal-rails: these were originally fitted with water-scoops and visible tank-vents. This equipment (including the vents) was removed in the 1930s.

2 4,125 gallons, almost identical to the above but the sides were higher.

3 4,125 gallons, 'self-trimming': these had the same outward appearance as 2 above but the insides of the coal-space sloped towards the footplate to enable the coal to gravitate down to the fireman, thus saving him a lot of walking as the tender emptied!

4 4,125 gallons, 'self-trimming', with curved rear ends to the coal-rails (as on the Nu-Cast 'Q6' and 'B16' kits).

5 4,125 gallons, 'self-trimming', with cut-back coal-rails; someone at Darlington got to work with an acetylene torch and removed the coal-rails from the rear of the tender to allow better access when taking water.

6 No 63400 was damaged in a collision during October 1957, and the tender was a 'write-off'. Darlington took the tender from a withdrawn 'D20' and put No 63400 back into traffic. This tender was one of a handful rebuilt during 1949/50 with straight sides, and saw service behind five 'Q6s' until it was scrapped in June 1966. During this nine-year spell No 63377 had it the longest (seven years), while second longest was No 63400 (only 12 months).

It is possible to rebuild the Hornby 'B17'/'D49' tender into all of these types as long as we put the difference in length (6mm) down to 'modeller's

licence'. The subject of my model, No 63417, had a tender with cut-back coal-rails, and the method of construction is as follows. First dismantle the rear of the tender (**Figure 20**), then replace the rear coal partition 5mm forward of its original position. Removing the LNER-pattern water-dome leaves a square hole in the coal-space; cover this with a piece of paper glued to its underside, then cover the paper with imitation coal. Next fit an NER-pattern water-filler in the same position as its 'B17' predecessor. I used a white-metal casting from Dave Alexander (from his 'Q6' kit). Then fit a round water-dome into the gap between the water-filler and the rear coal partition; again I used the white-metal casting from Dave Alexander's 'Q6 kit. Next manufacture new side-raves from card (**Figure 21**), and glue them to the tender with the top edges level with the top edges of the 'B17' tender.

Next manufacture the four coal-rails for each side of the tender from 1mm-diameter brass wire (available from Alan Gibson). Bend them to shape and glue them to the newly made side-

Figure 20: Modifications to Hornby 'B17' tender

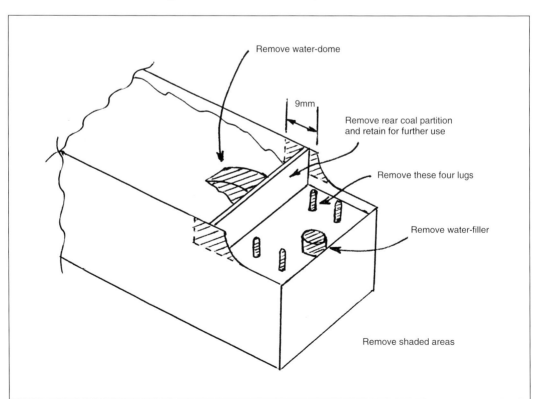

Remove water-dome

9mm

Remove rear coal partition and retain for further use

Remove these four lugs

Remove water-filler

Remove shaded areas

Figure 21: New side-raves for tender

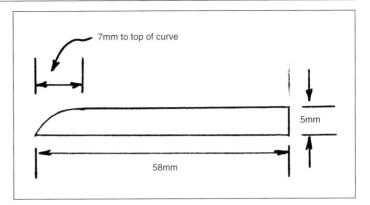

7mm to top of curve

5mm

58mm

The completed tender. Note the coal rails made from 1mm-diameter brass wire, producing a very pleasing result.

raves 1mm apart (use photographs as a guide). With this done the model is ready for painting and transfers; the livery carried in BR days was unlined black and the route availability was RA6. So there you have it – another useful addition to any LNER layout.

Ex-LNER 'O4/7' 2-8-0 No 63891

In 1939 Gresley rebuilt an ex-GCR 'O4/1' with a larger 5ft 6in-diameter boiler and round-topped firebox (as used on his 'O2' Class of 2-8-0s), while retaining the original smokebox, chassis and cab. Altogether 41 locos were rebuilt, the last being completed in 1947. During the late 1940s seven of them were further rebuilt by Edward Thompson, leaving 34 to soldier on as Gresley locos. They spent unspectacular lives, rarely venturing outside LNER territory, but, in common with the unrebuilt members of Class 'O4', they earned themselves a reputation for reliability and ruggedness. They could be seen anywhere on the Eastern Region, from Stratford in the south to Doncaster in the north. They could also be seen on ex-Great Central lines around Manchester, and six locos were allocated to the North Eastern Region: five to Dairycoates (53A) and one to Cudworth (53F). The class became extinct in December 1965 when No 63770 was withdrawn off Colwick (40E). A model of one of these locos would be a useful addition to any LNER layout.

Items required

Hornby '28xx' loco body and Margate chassis (*not* Chinese) (it is also possible to use the LMS 8F chassis); Hornby 8F tender chassis (including power unit); Hornby 'B17' boiler and smokebox; Hornby 'B17' or 'D49' tender body; detailing parts as described in text.

Stage 1: The loco chassis

The only modification required to the GWR '28xx' chassis is the removal of the 'firebox glow' assembly; because we are moving the cab further forward we have to dispense with this feature. If you are using the 8F chassis, also remove that assembly. Remove the 8F cylinders and motion from the chassis block, and with a hacksaw remove the top of the cylinder (valve-chests) from the cylinder block. Then file down the remains of each cylinder into a more circular profile. Next cut out two pieces of paper 14mm by 25mm and glue them in place, wrapped around each cylinder. When the glue has dried paint the cylinders black. Next, with a hacksaw, remove the combination-lever from each crosshead and slidebar assembly. Remove the rearmost of the two motion support brackets, and file down the top of the leading bracket until it is flush with the top of the chassis block. Now replace the slidebars, crossheads and connecting-rods – your chassis is now complete.

Stage 2: The loco body

First of all remove the GWR whistle, boiler handrails and reversing-rod. Then remove the struts connecting the underside of the smokebox to the buffer-beam. Remove the frames, steps and sandboxes from the underside of the cab, but leave the drag-beam intact (**Figure 2**). Retain the frames and sandboxes for further use. Next file or cut away the GWR numberplates from the cab sides, then remove the cab from the rest of the body by making a vertical hacksaw cut immediately in front of the cab (**Figure 2** again). Next remove the peculiar bracket from beneath the second splasher on the right-hand side of the loco. Remove the boiler, firebox and smokebox from the running-plate by making a horizontal cut through the firebox 4mm above the rear splashers – *make sure that this cut is straight and level, as the 'B17' boiler has to rest on this 'stump'*. Next cut through the two pipes leading from the

Above 'O4/7' 2-8-0 No 63582 at Bidston on 3 November 1956. *David Holmes*

Below The completed model of No 63891.

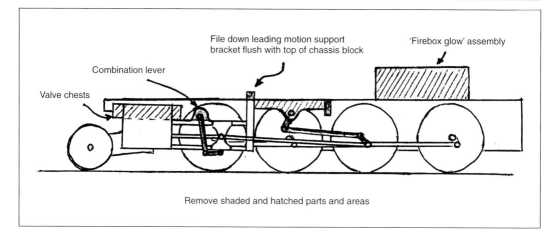

Above Figure 1: Modification to 8F chassis

Below The modified 8F chassis.

top-feed to the running-plate, then cut through the two circular boiler supports abaft the leading splashers – *take care not to damage the splashers.* Finally make a horizontal saw cut through the base of the smokebox saddle. Clean up any residue and rough edges with a file or emery-cloth.

If you are using the 8F chassis, part of the running-plate will have to be removed to accommodate the top of the motion support bracket, so cut or file a 4mm-wide socket in the underside of the running-plate (on both sides of the loco), 59mm from the front buffer-beam.

Now examine the underside of the cab and you will notice that the rear drag-beam has two square holes in it. When we shorten the body these will be utilised for holding the chassis locating lugs. However, first we need to remove the existing 'chassis location bracket' (**Figure 3**) – a craft-knife is the best tool for this job. When the bracket has been removed it is important to file away all of the residue to ensure that the body sits squarely on the chassis.

Now we have to do something about the buffer-beam and the front portion of the running-plate. The 'O4s' had a straight running-plate at buffer-beam level, whereas the running-plate of the '28xx' was slightly higher with a curved step to it – this needs to be camouflaged in some way! First, with the hacksaw, remove the buffers, then cut through each side of the running-plate horizontally at the top of each curve; take this cut as far as the raised section with the hole through it (**Figure 4**). Then make two further cuts through the front of the buffer-beam to link up with the first two (**Figure 4**

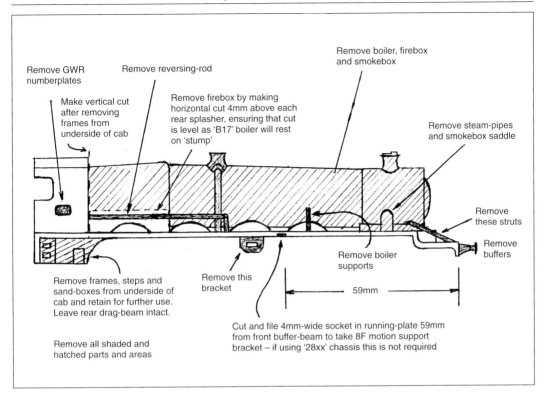

Remove GWR numberplates

Remove reversing-rod

Remove boiler, firebox and smokebox

Make vertical cut after removing frames from underside of cab

Remove firebox by making horizontal cut 4mm above each rear splasher, ensuring that cut is level as 'B17' boiler will rest on 'stump'

Remove steam-pipes and smokebox saddle

Remove these struts

Remove buffers

Remove boiler supports

Remove frames, steps and sand-boxes from underside of cab and retain for further use. Leave rear drag-beam intact.

Remove this bracket

59mm

Remove all shaded and hatched parts and areas

Cut and file 4mm-wide socket in running-plate 59mm from front buffer-beam to take 8F motion support bracket – if using '28xx' chassis this is not required

Above Figure 2: Modifications to '28xx' body

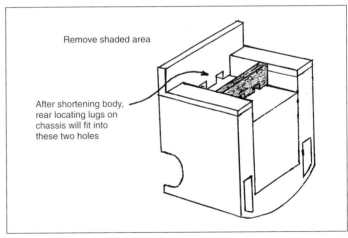

Remove shaded area

After shortening body, rear locating lugs on chassis will fit into these two holes

Right Figure 3: Underside of '28xx' cab

again). This will remove the two outside portions of the buffer-beam; shorten these two portions to a length of 13mm (again, see **Figure 4**). Remove the front 3mm from the central section of the buffer-beam, and clean up all of the sawn edges with a file or emery-cloth, paying particular attention to the remaining leading edge of the running-plate – *this needs to be filed square.*

Now, from card or Plasticard manufacture a new buffer-beam, 33mm by 7mm, and drill two 1.5mm-diameter holes on the horizontal centre-line 5mm from each outside edge (to take the buffers). Then drill a 1.5mm-diameter hole in the exact centre of the new buffer-beam (to take the coupling-hook). Reassemble the loco's front end as shown in **Figure 5**. When the glue has dried fill any gaps with Milliput or similar, including the large rectangular void in the centre.

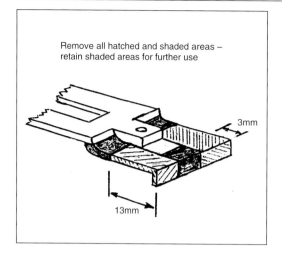

Remove all hatched and shaded areas –
retain shaded areas for further use

3mm

13mm

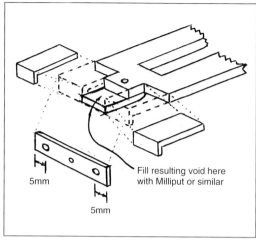

5mm

5mm

Fill resulting void here
with Milliput or similar

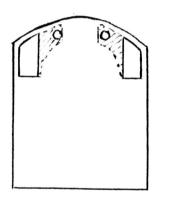

Remove shaded areas

Enlarge front windows with file or craft-knife as shown.
Radius of inside edges should match as closely as
possible profile of 'B17' boiler.

Above left Figure 4: Dissection of '28xx' front buffer-beam

Above Figure 5: Reassembly of front buffer-beam

Left Figure 6: Modifications to '28xx' cab front

while leaving the other boiler detail intact as far as possible (boiler-bands and washout plugs). Next remove all six splasher mouldings from the bottom of the boiler with a craft-knife, and clean up with a file or emery-cloth. Then fill in the remaining recesses with Milliput or similar. When the filler has set paint these areas black.

Next a word or two about the dome. Some members of this sub-class had the massive 'angular Gorton' version, while others had a more modern version very similar to that of the Hornby 'B17'. If the loco you are modelling carried one of the massive domes, now would be the time to remove the 'B17' example; this is easily done by inserting a screwdriver into either end of the boiler and just prising it out from underneath. However, I do not know of any manufacturer who produces a casting for one of the 'angular Gorton' domes, so retaining the 'B17' dome would be a safer option.

We now move on to the 'B17' smokebox. First remove the chimney, leaving the snifting-valve intact. Remove the vacuum-ejector pipe from the left-hand side, and the steam-pipes from both sides of the smokebox, and file any residue flush. Then file down the sides of the smokebox saddle to a vertical profile (**Figure 7**). Remove the screw-socket from the underside of the smokebox saddle, and finally remove the

Remove 5mm from the rear of the running-plate, ensuring that the cuts are straight and square as the resulting edges will have to fit square against the cab front when the two are glued together. Next enlarge the cab's front windows with a file or craft-knife (**Figure 6**). The radius of the curved inside edges needs to match (as near as possible) the profile of the 'B17' boiler (5ft 6in diameter).

We now turn our attention to the 'B17' boiler, and with the craft-knife remove the vacuum-ejector pipe from the left-hand side of the boiler. File any residue flush with a piece of emery-cloth,

Figure 7: Modifications to 'B17' smokebox

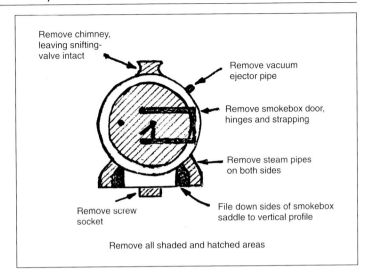

Remove chimney, leaving snifting-valve intact

Remove vacuum ejector pipe

Remove smokebox door, hinges and strapping

Remove steam pipes on both sides

Remove screw socket

File down sides of smokebox saddle to vertical profile

Remove all shaded and hatched areas

smokebox door, its hinges and strapping. I achieved this by drilling out the centre, starting with a 1.5mm-diameter drill, and working up in stages to a 10mm-diameter drill. Doing this job in stages prevents the plastic from splitting! Then I used a craft-knife to remove the remains of the door, and finally removed the hinges with a file (also **Figure 7**).

A white-metal casting for a Great Central smokebox door is available from Craftsman Models Ltd (from their 'A5' kit). This is a very good casting and comes complete with a handle (dart), although for an 'O4/7' a horizontal handrail needs to be added (use photographs as a guide). With this done, glue the new door in place, then glue the boiler to the smokebox – *ensure that the dome and snifting-valve are correctly aligned*. When the glue has dried test-fit the 'B17' boiler to the '28xx' running-plate. You will find that the smokebox needs an extra 3mm adding to its base. On my model I used three pieces of 1mm-thick Plasticard 16mm wide by 18mm long, gluing them one on top of the other to the underside of the smokebox saddle. With this extra 3mm added, the boiler should fit straight and level on the running-plate. When you are satisfied, glue the two parts together. When the glue has set fill in any gaps in the firebox join with Milliput or similar.

At this point it would be a good idea to add some extra weight inside the boiler; this will make the driving wheels 'bite' and improve the electrical contacts. I used half a dozen 3-inch nails wrapped in masking-tape, and packed into the boiler with pieces of kitchen-roll for a tight fit! If you don't have any nails handy, exhausted 'AA'-size batteries are quite useful for this type of job.

Now a word or two about the chimney. The 'O4/7s' were fitted with Great Central lipped chimneys 15 inches tall (as fitted to the 'D10s', the first 11 'D11s', some of the 'A5s' and some of the Great Central 4-6-0s). Unfortunately I do not know of any manufacturer who produces a casting for one of these chimneys! On my model I used a Jackson-Evans 'Black Five' chimney and filed away part of it with a small round file (**Figure 8**). When you are satisfied with the new profile, glue the chimney in the same position as its 'B17' predecessor, at the same time ensuring that it is in line with the snifting valve and dome.

We now turn our attention to the '28xx' cab. We need to fill in the inside of the boiler backhead with Milliput or similar, or cover it with paper or thin card. With this done, glue the cab to the firebox and running-plate, while at the same time ensuring that the ensemble is straight and square. When the glue has dried plug any gaps with Milliput or similar. Then, with a craft-knife or file, remove the raised edges of the cab roof.

Next manufacture the combined splashers for the rear six wheels from card or Plasticard (**Figure 9**), then glue them in place over the existing splashers. Now manufacture the

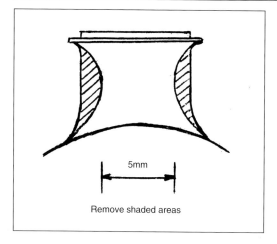

Figure 8: Modification of 'Black Five' chimney

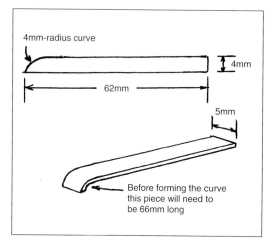

Figure 9: Combined splashers for rear three axles

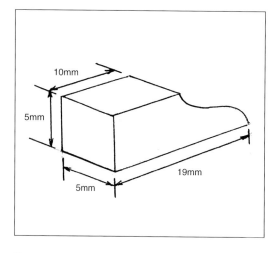

Figure 10: New combined front splashers and sand-boxes

combined splashers and sandboxes for the front driving wheels (**Figure 10**), then glue them in place over the existing splashers. From a piece of scrap brass or microstrip, manufacture a reversing-rod 2mm wide by 59mm long and glue it to the right-hand side of the loco with the rear end 7mm above the splasher, and the leading end hidden behind the curved part of the main splasher (use photographs as a guide).

Using card or Plasticard, manufacture the frame extensions (**Figure 11**). Glue the shorter pair to the inside edges of the first and second splashers on each side of the loco (**Figure 12**), and the longer ones to the outside edges of the smokebox saddle on each side of the loco with their pointed ends in line with the top edge of the buffer-beam (also **Figure 12**). Manufacture the 'piano-front' from two rectangular pieces of card 16mm by 5mm and 15mm by 5mm, and glue them in place between the frame extensions directly in front of the smokebox (again see **Figure 12**). Then take two 23mm lengths of 3mm square microstrip and glue them to each side of the front frame extensions, with their rear ends butting onto the leading sandboxes, and their leading ends in line with the front of the smokebox (**Figure 12** again).

Now fit a Wakefield mechanical lubricator to the left-hand running-plate immediately behind the leading splasher, backing onto the frame extension (use photographs as a guide). Cut two lengths of 1mm-diameter wire, 8mm long, and glue in place between the top and bottom edges of the cab-side driver's cut-outs. Fit the whistle and Ross 'pop' safety-valves into their respective sockets on the top of the 'B17' firebox (these items are available from a multitude of suppliers). Then fit the front lamp-brackets (available from Westward and South Eastern Finecast), using photographs as a guide for positioning these.

We now turn our attention to the frames that we removed from the underside of the '28xx' cab – these can be re-used on the 'O4/7'. First remove the rear 8mm (including the GWR-style steps) with the craft-knife, then, *dependent on the chosen identity of your model*, remove the sandboxes (on rebuilding some locos had their rear sandboxes moved inside the cab – but not all of them – use a photograph as a guide). With this

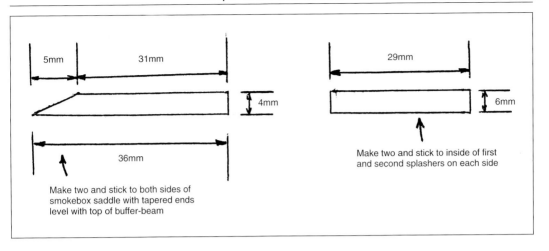

Above Figure 11: Manufacture of frame extensions

Below Figure 12: Front-end detail

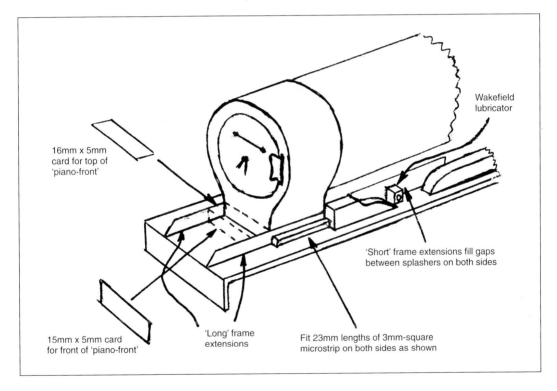

done glue the frames to the underside of the cab 20mm apart so that the chassis can fit between them. When the glue has dried add a pair of cab steps; Great Central pattern steps are difficult to find, but Stanier LMS ones are not too far out. I used a pair of Stanier steps from Jackson-Evans, and they don't look too bad.

Next fit the boiler handrails. Note that on the 'O4/7s' they were not continuous (again use photographs as a guide). Fit a front coupling-hook (available from Mainly Trains and W&T Manufacturing) and a pair of Great Central-pattern oval buffers (these are available from Craftsman Models). Finally, *dependent on the chosen identity of your model*, fit a vacuum brake-pipe onto the front buffer-beam, together with a vacuum-ejector pipe along the right-hand side of the loco running from the cab to the middle of the smokebox (use thick wire or plastic rod). Note that not all 'O4/7s' were fitted with vacuum brakes, so work from a photograph of your chosen subject. The loco body is now ready for painting; the livery carried in both LNER and BR days was unlined black.

Stage 3: The tender

First, with the craft-knife, remove the two lugs from the underside of the tender front. Then remove the water-filler and the four lugs (used for locating the vacuum-tanks) from the rear of the tender, and file flush as best you can without damaging the outside rim of the tender. Next remove the water-dome from the coal space, then remove the rear coal partition (take care not to damage it as it will be re-used). Remove the rear 5mm of the tender tops (**Figure 13**). Glue the rear coal partition further forward (at the rear edge of the coal), then cut out a piece of paper 15mm square and glue it to the underside of the hole left by the removal of the water-dome. When the glue has set camouflage the hole with imitation coal, and paint it black. Cut out a piece of paper 30mm by 21mm and glue it over the top of the water tank.

Manufacture a pair of tender tops from card or Plasticard (**Figure 14**), and glue them to the outside edges of the tender tops to give the impression of stepped-out sides. Manufacture a new water-filler (**Figure 15**) from card, Plasticard, or even wood. Next glue a length of 1mm square microstrip around the top back edge of the tender to create the impression of a flared top.

In order to make the LNER 'D49' tender body fit the LMS 8F tender chassis, the six locating-lugs on the tender frame need to be reduced in size (the LNER tender body appears to be narrower than its LMS counterpart). Once this has been done, fit a pair of Hornby oval buffers and your model is complete! The route availability was RA6.

Figure 13: Modifications to tender body

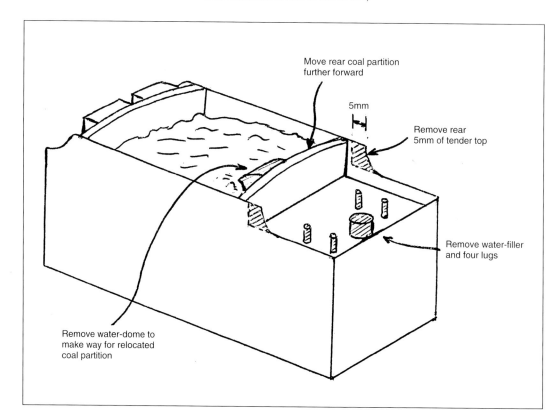

Move rear coal partition further forward

5mm

Remove rear 5mm of tender top

Remove water-filler and four lugs

Remove water-dome to make way for relocated coal partition

Figure 14: Manufacture of new tender tops

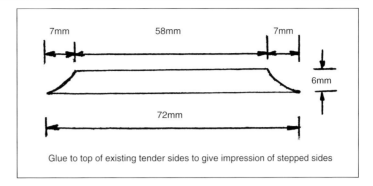

Glue to top of existing tender sides to give impression of stepped sides

Figure 15: Manufacture of new tender water-filler

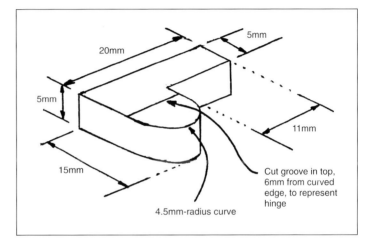

The completed tender.

Ex-LNER 'J11/3' 0-6-0 No 64406

In 1942 Edward Thompson decided to rebuild the ex-Great Central Class 'J11' into a new 'LNER Standard Class', with the slide-valves of the originals replaced by piston-valves. The increased size of these new piston-valves necessitated the boiler pitch being raised by 4 inches, which in turn resulted in the boiler mountings being reduced in height. The original intention was to equip these rebuilds with round-top fireboxes, but for economy reasons (it was the middle of the war, after all) this modification was not carried out.

The rebuilding of the locos into Class 'J11/3', as the rebuilds became known, continued until 1953 when, with the onset of dieselisation, it was considered uneconomical to carry on. Up to this point 31 locos had been rebuilt, and they spent all of their careers allocated to ex-Great Central sheds, not only working freight trains but also on some passenger diagrams, where they regularly put up good performances. They were also utilised for seaside excursions, which sometimes took them to destinations outside GCR territory. I have in my possession a photograph of No 64417 climbing Enthorpe Bank unassisted with nine carriages forming an excursion from Manchester to Bridlington and Filey.

The first 'J11/3s' to be withdrawn were Nos 64439 and 64441, which went in February 1961; the last to be withdrawn was No 64354 in October 1962.

Items required

Hornby/Dapol/Airfix LMS 4F; detailing parts as described in text.

Stage 1: The loco body

First of all separate the loco body from the chassis; this is held in place by two screws, one at each end of the chassis. Remove the cab, which is only a 'clip-fit' and can be removed with a penknife blade. Then remove the whistle and safety-valves, together with the 'Midland-style' vacuum-ejector pipe (a plastic moulding on the left-hand side of the boiler) and its associated pipework. Remove the boiler handrails, the vacuum-pipe and both mechanical lubricators from the right-hand running-plate. With the hacksaw, remove the dome and chimney, then file the remains flush with the boiler. Undo the two screws on the underside of the body that hold the lead weight in place, then insert a screwdriver or penknife blade between the rear of the lead weight and the rear of the firebox and prise the weight forwards against the smokebox door; it will then come away, being only glued in place – retain the lead weight for further use. Next, with a craft-knife or hacksaw, remove the raised centre part of the buffer-beam together with the 'piano-front'. Again with the craft-knife, remove the reversing-rod – take extra care with its removal as it can be re-used for the 'J11'.

Now a word or two about the cab and firebox. The 'J11' cabs completely enclosed the rear pair of driving wheels, but if we do this on the model we will end up with a ridiculously short firebox. We shall therefore have to invoke a bit of 'modeller's licence' and compromise. I decided to make the cab 23mm in length (**Figure 2**). This provides a substantial cab, while still leaving a reasonably sized firebox. So, from 1mm thick card or Plasticard, manufacture the sides and front of the new cab (**Figures 1 and 2**). Manufacturing the new cab, including the

Above 'J11/3' 0-6-0 No 64442, paired with 'K3' 2-6-0 No 61943, on a working for which these engines were sometimes used – the 9.32am additional Skegness-Barnsley train – having arrived at Barnsley Exchange at 12.54pm on 26 August 1961. *David Holmes*

Below The completed model of No 64406.

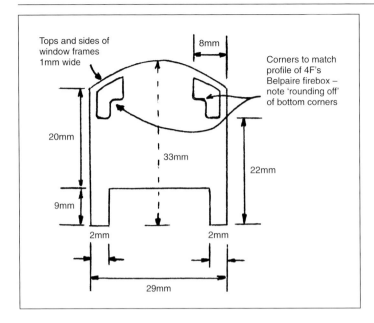

Tops and sides of window frames 1mm wide

8mm

Corners to match profile of 4F's Belpaire firebox – note 'rounding off' of bottom corners

20mm

33mm

22mm

9mm

2mm   2mm

29mm

Left Figure 1: New cab front

Below left Figure 2: New cab sides

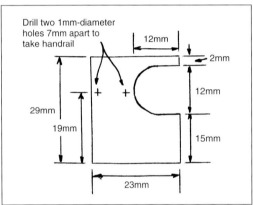

Drill two 1mm-diameter holes 7mm apart to take handrail

12mm

2mm

12mm

29mm

19mm

15mm

23mm

carving out of the front windows, is the hardest part of this conversion; once done, the rest is plain sailing!

Once you have made the parts for the new cab, cut a 1mm-wide vertical slot through the top of the firebox (to take the new cab front); take this slot down as far as the top of the rear splasher on each side of the firebox (**Figure 3**). Test-fit the new cab front in the slot for a straight and square fit and, when satisfied, glue in place.

Fit the cab-side handrails and glue the new cab sides into position. The slot for the new cab front will have cut through the centre of the

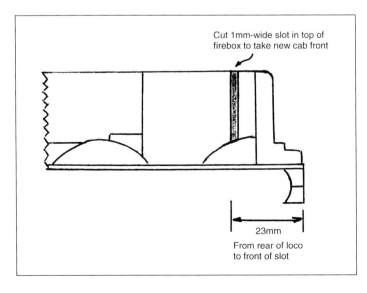

Cut 1mm-wide slot in top of firebox to take new cab front

23mm

From rear of loco to front of slot

Left Figure 3: Modifications to rear of firebox

raised safety-valve mounting, so file away the rest of it and we will be left with a 1mm-diameter hole 3mm forward of the new cab front (we can use this hole for the whistle – re-use that of the 4F). Next drill two further 1mm-diameter holes, on the centre-line, the first 3mm forward of the whistle, the second 5mm ahead of the first. Re-fit the 4F safety-valves into these holes.

We now turn our attention to the front end of the loco. When we removed the raised portion of the buffer-beam (in front of the smokebox) we were left with a rectangular hole. Fill this with Milliput or similar, and while the filler is setting insert a Westward lamp-bracket into the filler, in line with the front coupling. Next drill two 1mm-diameter holes through the front running-plate above each buffer, and fit a Westward lamp-bracket into each hole. Next fit a Wakefield lubricator to the left-hand running-plate immediately to the rear of the leading splasher (be careful and work from a photograph – while the majority of 'J11s' had their lubricators on the left-hand side, a few had them fitted on the right).

Next, with Milliput or similar, fill in the hole left by the removal of the dome, and at the same time fill in the sandbox fillers on each side of the firebox. When the filler has set, file flush with emery-cloth. Now move on to the boiler mountings (chimney, dome and snifting-valves); suitable castings for the 'J11/3' are available from Alan Gibson (and they are of very good quality). First fit the chimney in the same position as its LMS predecessor, then fit the snifting-valve directly behind the chimney. Next fit the dome abaft the second boiler-band, and check that all three fittings are square and in line. With the hacksaw, remove 12mm from the rear of the 4F's lead-weight, and fix it back in place inside the boiler.

Alan Gibson also produces a complete smokebox front for a 'J11/3', which includes the GCR smokebox door, the valve-chest covers, and the valve tail-rods (another very good casting – and it saves the loco-builder a lot of work!). If you are planning to use a Markits smokebox door handle, you will need to drill a 1.5mm-diameter hole through the centre of the smokebox door. Once you've assembled the smokebox front and glued it in place, fill any gaps around its base with Milliput or similar.

The front of the model, showing the white-metal smokebox door casting and the front of the valve-chests (including tail-rods). The numberplate is an SMS transfer, sadly no longer available. The other transfers are by Modelmaster.

Next, from a piece of scrap brass or microstrip 1mm wide by 40mm long, manufacture a reversing-rod (use photographs as a guide). If you managed to remove the 4F's reversing-rod without damaging it, you could incorporate it into the new loco. From a 73mm-long piece of 1mm-diameter wire or plastic rod, manufacture the vacuum-ejector pipe and glue it to the right-hand side of the boiler just above the handrail (use photographs as a guide). From an 88mm length of 1mm-diameter wire, manufacture the cab rear handrails. Bend the wire to shape using the cab front as a guide, then glue the wire to the rear of the cab. Next, from a piece of card 25mm by 35mm, manufacture the cab-roof; bend it to shape and glue it in place. Manufacture the roof ribs from 1mm square microstrip, again using photographs as a guide because while the majority of locos had three transverse ribs, some only had two. Next fit the boiler handrail (yet again use photographs as a guide), and your model is now ready for painting. The livery in BR days was unlined black. Finally glue the 4F vacuum-pipe back in its original position, and the loco is ready for the fixing of transfers.

Stage 2: The tender-body

First of all remove the water-filler and dome from the rear of the tender. I find that the easiest way of doing this is to drill them out: start off with a small size drill (say 2mm diameter) and work up in stages (in the case of the dome to 8mm diameter). If you don't do it in stages and try to use the large drills first you may crack the plastic. With this done, file any residue flush with the tank top, then cover the top with a piece of paper

27mm by 22mm glued in place. Manufacture a Great Central-style combined water-dome and filler (**Figure 4**) from card, wood or balsa-wood, or even five layers of 1mm-thick Plasticard, and glue in place as shown in **Figure 6**.

Next, from card or Plasticard, manufacture new side-raves (**Figure 5**) and glue them over the existing side-raves to give the impression of a stepped tender (**Figure 6**). Add lengths of 1mm square microstrip around the rear of the tender to give the impression of a flared edge (**Figure 6** again).

Your model is now ready for painting. The livery carried both in LNER and BR days was unlined black, and the route availability was RA5.

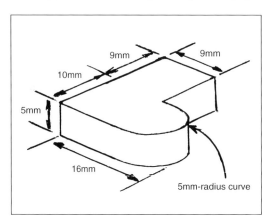

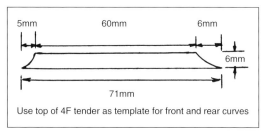

Use top of 4F tender as template for front and rear curves

Left Figure 4: GCR-style combined water-dome and filler

Above Figure 5: Manufacture of new side-raves

Below Figure 6: Reassembly of tender

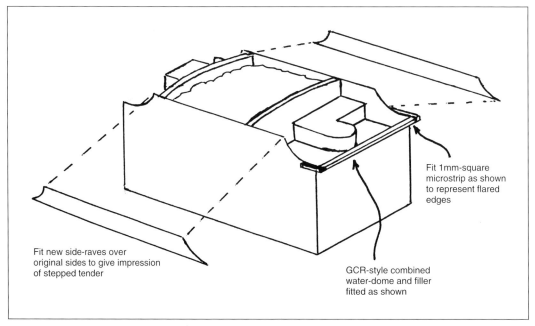

Fit new side-raves over original sides to give impression of stepped tender

Fit 1mm-square microstrip as shown to represent flared edges

GCR-style combined water-dome and filler fitted as shown

Ex-LNER 'J19' 0-6-0 No 64655

In 1934 someone at the LNER (probably A. H. Peppercorn, but maybe even Gresley himself) decided to fit an ex-Great Eastern Railway Class 'J19' 0-6-0 with a Class 'B17' boiler, as had already been done with Classes 'B12' and 'D16', bringing about dramatic improvements to their performance. The rebuilding of the 'J19' must have been a success because by 1939 the other 24 members of the class had been so treated, together with the 10 members of the almost identical Class 'J18', to make up a 35-strong class. All 35 locos survived into nationalisation and two (Nos 64657/64664) survived until the end of steam on the Great Eastern in September 1962.

Many years ago I read about Crownline Ltd producing a Great Eastern tender kit to fit around the Hornby 'Patriot' tender-drive power unit in order to convert the Hornby 'B17' into one of the early examples with the small GE tender. Given all the foregoing information I arrived at the following formula: Hornby 'B12' tender + Hornby 'Patriot' power unit + Hornby 'B17' loco body + 4F loco chassis + 4F running-plate and splashers = LNER 'J19'. Here's how I did it.

Items required

Hornby 'B12' tender; Hornby 'Patriot' drive unit (X1075); Hornby 'B17' loco body; Class 4F loco body and chassis; two 6BA screws; one 4BA washer.

Stage 1: The tender

First of all completely dismantle the 'B12' tender and remove sufficient material from the tender floor/underframe to clear the motor housing and gears of the power unit. Next drill a 2mm-diameter hole 12mm from the front of the tender-frame (**Figure 1**). Remove the wheels from the front (stepped) end of the 'Patriot' power unit and remove the 'step' with a hacksaw (**Figure 2**). With this done replace the front wheels, remove the rear wheels and remove 3mm from the rear of the power unit (**also Figure 2**). Test-fit to the tender frame, and keep filing until the power unit fits inside the tender frame – make sure that the rear wheels are clear of the coupling.

Next, with the power unit in place inside the tender frame, fit a 6BA screw into the hole that you have drilled through the frame to hold the frame and power unit together. Fit the second 6BA screw and the 4BA washer into the rear hole of the power unit; you will find that the washer overlaps the edge of the tender frame and holds the power unit and tender frame firmly together. Next remove the screw/bolt housing from inside the tender body, then remove the part of the tender body underneath the footplate, to allow passage of the wires from loco to power unit (**Figure 3**).

Stage 2: The 4F body

First remove the body from the chassis (it is held in place by two screws, one at each end of the chassis). Then remove the cab (it clip-fits on to the footplate, so a penknife should do it). With a hacksaw or craft-knife, remove the boiler and reversing-rod from the running-plate and splashers, *leaving behind 9mm of the firebox and the smokebox saddle* (**Figure 4**). Next remove the raised platform in front of the reverser handle in the cab (also **Figure 4**). Retain the safety-valves, whistle and lead weight for further use.

Above 'J19' 0-6-0 No 64669 at March on 1 August 1960. *David Holmes*

Below The completed model of No 64655.

Figure 1: Plan of Hornby 'B12' tender underframe

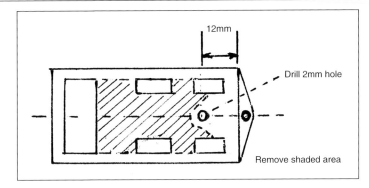

Figure 2: Hornby 'Patriot' power unit (X1075)

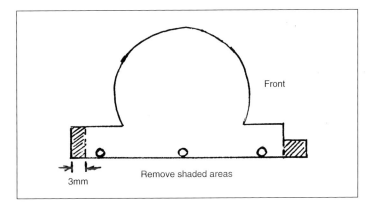

The Hornby 'B12' tender underframe and 'Patriot' power unit assembled together. Note the two 6BA screws and 4BA washer.

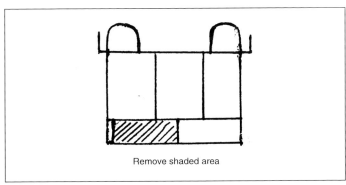

Figure 3: Front view of Hornby 'B12' tender body

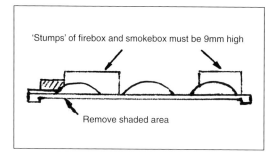

Figure 4: Bottom half of 4F body

Stage 3: The 'B17' body

The Hornby 'B17' body comes in three separate parts – cab, boiler and smokebox – which makes modification easier. First of all remove 5mm from the bottom of the cab plus the 'firing well' and firehole door, but *leave the cab side-sheets intact* (**Figure 5**). With these modifications the 'B17' cab should fit onto the rear of the 4F running-plate.

Next remove 25mm from the 'B17' boiler. First cut through the boiler just in front of the rearmost boiler-band, with the second cut 25mm forward of the first (**Figure 6**). Then, with a craft-knife, remove the regulator (vacuum-ejector) pipe from the remains of the boiler; the 'J19s' were all right-hand drive, whereas the 'B17s' were left-hand. Remove all of the remaining splashers from the 'B17' boiler and fill in the resulting holes in the bottom of the boiler with filler reinforced with paper (ie paper stuck on the inside of boiler with filler on top). When the filler has set, file flush.

We next turn our attention to the smokebox.

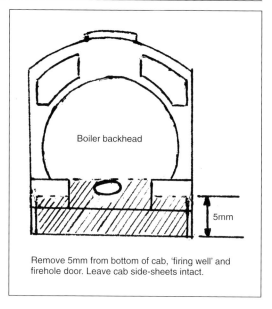

Remove 5mm from bottom of cab, 'firing well' and firehole door. Leave cab side-sheets intact.

Figure 5: Rear view of 'B17' cab

First, with the craft-knife, remove the regulator (vacuum-ejector) pipe from the side of the smokebox. Now we need to make a decision about the chimney: do we want to retain the Hornby moulding or fit a better one (many of which are available on the market)? The 'J19s' had a standard LNER 'flower-pot' as carried by the 'D16s', 'D49s' and 'J39s', among others. If you want to change the chimney this is the best point to remove the old one; however, *take care not to damage the snifting-valve in the process*. Next remove the steam-pipes and saddle from the underside of the smokebox, and file the underside smooth (**Figure 7**).

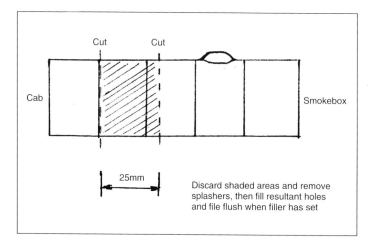

Figure 6: 'B17' boiler

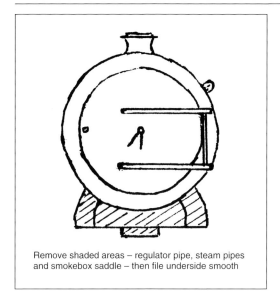

Remove shaded areas – regulator pipe, steam pipes and smokebox saddle – then file underside smooth

Figure 7: 'B17' smokebox

Stage 4: The 'J19' body

Stick together the two remaining parts of the 'B17' boiler and ensure that they are correctly aligned. While the glue is setting, remove 5mm from the lead weight of the 4F with a hacksaw. When the glue has set, place the lead weight inside the boiler and secure with Milliput or similar. Next attach the 'B17' cab to the rear of the boiler in such a way that the forward protrusions fit around the lead weight. As the 'B17' cab is wider than that of the 4F, the latter's running-plate needs to be widened at the cab end. Stick a piece of card or thin Plasticard 21mm long and 3mm wide on each side, at the rear end of the 4F's running-plate, in order to support the new cab. Remove the 4F's front steps and file smooth; the 'J19s', in common with all other ex-Great Eastern 0-6-0s, did not have front steps!

Now return to the 'B17' boiler and cab. When the glue and filler has set and the lead weight is nicely secured in place, glue the smokebox to the boiler, ensuring that everything is square and in line. Next stick a piece of card or Plasticard across the remains of the 4F firebox to form a platform on which the 'B17' boiler will sit. When the glue has set, offer the 'B17' boiler/cab/smokebox to the '4F' running-plate. Check that the top of the boiler is level and

straight; if not, use scrap pieces of card, for example, under the smokebox or firebox until it is level. When you are satisfied, glue the cab/boiler and smokebox to the 4F's running-plate, check that everything is square, straight and level, and put aside to dry.

When the glue has dried fill in all gaps in the boiler, the bottom of the cab, the joins between the smokebox and saddle, and the join at the bottom of the firebox. On the firebox join I used a couple of pieces of paper (ever heard the saying 'Papering over the cracks'?); the final result isn't too bad, especially after a couple of coats of paint to strengthen it. Don't forget to fill in the front of the firebox underneath the boiler.

Stage 5: Detailing the body

If you have opted to fit a replacement chimney, this is a good time to fit it. Next manufacture two rear sandboxes from card or Plasticard, 3mm deep by 9.5mm square, then do the same for the two centre sandboxes – 3mm deep by 6.5mm square. Glue them in place as per the photographs. Next manufacture a regulator (vacuum-ejector) pipe from heavy-gauge wire or plastic-rod 73mm long, and stick in place on the right-hand side of loco, 2.5mm above the boiler handrail. Manufacture a reversing-rod from scrap brass or microstrip 51mm long and 1.5mm wide, and glue to the right-hand side of the loco. The rear end of the rod should be fixed 5mm below the boiler handrail and the front end should be fixed behind the centre sandbox; again, use the photographs as a guide.

Fit medium-sized handrail knobs into the existing holes in the 'B17' boiler, then thread through the handrail wire. Fit the safety-valves and whistle from the 4F, the vacuum-pipes and the cab footsteps. Next manufacture the front sandboxes and splashers from card or Plasticard (**Figure 8**), and glue them in place as per the photographs.

Manufacture the 'piano-front' cover from card or Plasticard (**Figure 9**). Next take a wooden cocktail-stick or 1mm-diameter plastic rod, cut two pieces 1mm long and glue them to the front of the 'piano-front' (also **Figure 9**). When the glue has set stick the 'piano-front' over the raised central portion of the 4F's front running-plate, as

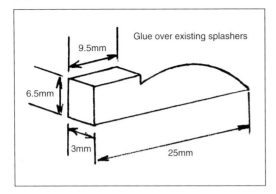

Above Figure 8: Class 'J19' combined
front sand-box and splasher

Below Figure 9: 'J19' 'piano-front' cover

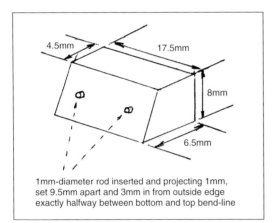

1mm-diameter rod inserted and projecting 1mm,
set 9.5mm apart and 3mm in from outside edge
exactly halfway between bottom and top bend-line

per the photographs. Finally glue a Wakefield lubricator to the leading side of the centre sandbox on the right-hand side of the loco, again using the photographs as a guide.

Stage 6: The final touches

Manufacture a tender drawbar from wire or scrap brass; being an 0-6-0 with a short-wheelbase tender you shouldn't need to worry about track radii. My model has the loco and tender coupled together as closely as possible and it still negotiates Peco Streamline small-radius points and Hornby second-radius curves. Hopefully your 4F loco chassis has plenty of wire attached to it, so that all you have to do to get it operational is to solder the wires from the loco chassis to the terminal on the power unit (and if you get the wires right first time you're very lucky!).

When the loco is running satisfactorily you can fit a vacuum-pipe to the rear of the tender, together with fire-irons, crew and transfers. Be careful when selecting an identity for your loco, as some members of the class ran with weather-boards on the front of their tenders, namely Nos 64662/63/64/65/70, according to the RCTS 'Green Book', Part 5. The 'J19s' were good-looking and useful locos, and one would be a handy addition to any Great Eastern layout.

Ex-SR 'T9' 4-4-0 No 30300

In 1899 the London & South Western Railway introduced its 'T9' Class of 4-4-0 express passenger locomotives. They were designed by Dugald Drummond, employed a 4ft 5in-diameter boiler, two inside cylinders, and 6ft 7in-diameter driving wheels. The locos were built in three batches, the first of which was constructed by Dubs & Co of Glasgow, and totalled 31 locos numbered 702-719 and 721-733. The second batch was built at the Nine Elms workshops of the LSWR, and totalled 20 locos, Nos 113-122 and 280-289. All of these 51 locos were fitted with narrow cabs and splashers. A third batch of 15 locos was built at Nine Elms and numbered 300-305/307/310-14/336-38, making a total for the class of 66 locos). This last batch of locos were fitted with wide cabs and splashers.

All of the Dubs-built locos, and the '300' series locos, were originally fitted with transverse firebox water-tubes, but this feature was removed by Urie in the early 1920s. All 66 locos were originally fitted with a Drummond-pattern lipped chimney, and his distinctive 'smokebox wing-plates'. During the 1920s Urie fitted superheaters to the whole class, which necessitated a forward extension of the smokebox, together with the removal of the wing-plates. At the same time the opportunity was taken to fit Urie's much-favoured 'stovepipe' design of chimney to all members of the class.

All 66 locos were fitted with vacuum brakes, while the last two to be built (Nos 337 and 338) were originally dual-braked (vacuum and Westinghouse – two brake-pipes on each buffer-beam and a pump mounted on the left-hand running-plate at the side of the smokebox). However, the Westinghouse equipment was removed from these two locos during 1934/5. As regards tenders, all of the Dubs-built locos

together with the first 20 of the Nine Elms-built examples were originally coupled to six-wheel tenders, while the last 15 (300 series) were given eight-wheel 'water-cart' tenders. Between 1902 and 1907 the first 51 locos were also given eight-wheel tenders (their six-wheel tenders being transferred to newly built Class 'K10' and 'L11' locos). Therefore all 66 'T9s' ran with eight-wheel tenders between 1907 and 1923.

The T9s were very successful engines, and proved very popular with their crews. They could be seen on all parts of the LSWR from Waterloo in the east to Padstow in the west. After the Grouping of 1923 the 'T9s' were tried out on other divisions of the Southern with immediate success, although with their eight-wheel tenders they proved to be too long for many of the turntables on the South Eastern Division. This led to 16 members of the class being coupled to six-wheel tenders purloined from 'K10s' and 'Black Motors'. During the Maunsell era all 66 'T9s' were fitted with his distinctive pattern of snifting-valve (one on each side of the smokebox), but these were all removed before nationalisation at Bulleid's instruction.

In the immediate post-war period 13 members of the class were fitted for oil-burning: Nos 113/114/115/118/121/280/286/303/305/314/713/722/731. In addition to the distinctive oil-tank on top of the tender, these locomotives were fitted with Bulleid-style ladders on the rear of the tenders, which were very similar to those on the new Bulleid 'Pacifics' then coming on stream. These 13 locos were also fitted with electric headlamps powered by a Stones generator (as fitted to the Bulleid 'Pacifics' and the more modern LNER locos around this time), which was sited on the left-hand running-plate at the side of the smokebox. Unfortunately the

Above One of the last seven 'T9' 4-4-0s to make it into the 1960s was No 30715, one of the original Dubs-built batch with narrow cab and splashers, seen here at the head of the 2.00pm Bodmin North-Padstow train at Wadebridge on 30 June 1960. *David Holmes*

Below The completed model. The transfers are a mixture of Modelmaster, SMS and Fox.

oil-burning experiment was terminated in October 1948, and all of the Southern Region's oil-burning locomotives (including the 13 'T9s') were put into store awaiting a drop in oil prices (which, of course, never came!). They were all condemned for scrap in the spring of 1951.

The 13 oil-burners were the first members of the class to be condemned. In fact, 1951 was a very bad year for the class, with a total of 20 being condemned. Electrification and dieselisation saw them ousted from the Central and South Eastern Divisions during the 1950s, and by the beginning of 1962 there were only seven left – Nos 30117 and 30287 at Eastleigh (71A), and Nos 30120, 30313, 30709, 30715 and 30717 all at Exmouth Junction (72A). The last one to be withdrawn was No 30120 in July 1963, but happily this engine is now preserved.

In its heyday this long-lived class (64 years) could be seen on all parts of the Southern Railway (and Southern Region in BR days). If your layout is based on the South Western Division one of these is a must!

Items required

Hornby/Dapol/Mainline ex-LMS 2P, complete loco and tender; detailing parts as described in the text.

Stage 1: Dissection of the loco body

First of all separate the loco body from the chassis; they are held together by a screw underneath the cab and a screw at the front end, which also holds the bogie in place. Then remove the cab; this is a separate moulding that is glued in place, and gentle coaxing with a penknife blade should remove it. With the cab gone it is now possible to remove the smokebox door – a gentle push from behind with a pen or pencil should do the trick! Next remove the LMS-style vacuum-ejector from the left-hand side of the smokebox (**Figure 1**); again, a penknife blade should lift it off. Also remove the reversing-rod and both mechanical lubricators, again using a penknife blade. Remove the whistle and safety-valves with a pair of pliers, then, with a hacksaw, remove the chimney and dome.

As we will be doing a bit of work on the loco's front end later (smokebox door, lamp-brackets, etc), it may be an idea to remove the front vacuum-pipe for safe keeping. As the 'T9s' all had continuous boiler handrails we shall have to remove the 2P's handrails (leave the knobs in place, however – we can re-employ them on the new model); a penknife blade and a pair of pliers should do the job.

Figure 1: 2P loco body after removal of cab

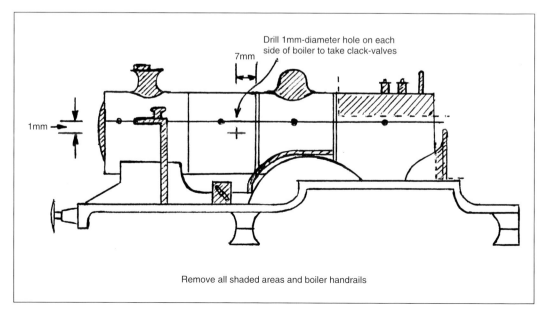

Drill 1mm-diameter hole on each side of boiler to take clack-valves

7mm

1mm

Remove all shaded areas and boiler handrails

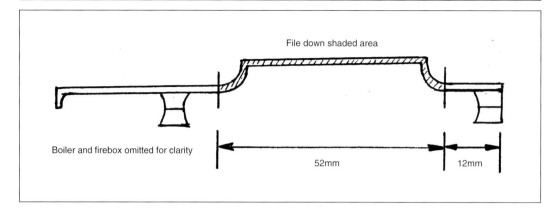

File down shaded area

Boiler and firebox omitted for clarity

52mm   12mm

Figure 2: Modifications to running-plate

Next remove the top of the Belpaire firebox with two horizontal hacksaw cuts just above the handrail knobs on each side of the firebox, and a vertical saw cut as near as possible to the front of the firebox without damaging the adjacent boiler-band (again, see **Figure 1**). Clean up the edges of the saw cuts with a file or emery-cloth. Now file or cut away the hind portions of the rear splashers so that their rear edges are in line with that of the firebox (**Figure 1** again). Then drill a 1mm-diameter hole through each side of the boiler 7mm ahead of the centre boiler-band, and 1mm below the level of the boiler handrails (to take the clack-valves – again see **Figure 1**). While you've got the drill out you might as well drill three more 1mm-diameter holes through the running-plate just above the buffer-beam to take the lamp-brackets, one directly above the coupling-hook and the other two 3mm in from the outside edges. Finally file away 1mm from the outside edges of the raised portions of the running-plate (including the quadrants) in readiness for fitting the new splasher casings (**Figure 2**).

Stage 2: Reassembling the loco body

Start the reassembly of the loco-body by filling in (with Milliput or similar) the holes left by the removal of the chimney, mechanical lubricators and vacuum-ejector. Then fill in the socket in the side of the boiler formerly occupied by the reversing-rod. Cut out a rectangle of card 26mm by 26mm to form the new (round) top for the firebox, bend it to shape and glue it in place. Then cut out a piece of paper to cover the firebox (**Figure 3**), thus hiding the joins and the 'threepenny-bit effect' on the top of the firebox. Use PVA adhesive for this job – it soaks into the paper and sets 'rock hard', creating a much stronger assembly.

Next, from card or 1mm-thick Plasticard, manufacture a new cab front (**Figure 4**) and glue it to the rear edge of the firebox, ensuring that the cut-out at the bottom clears the rear driving wheels. We now need to extend the smokebox by 4mm, so cut out two 22mm-diameter discs of 2mm-thick card or Plasticard, and glue them both to the front of the smokebox, thus lengthening it by 4mm. Then cut out a strip of paper 72mm long by 6mm wide and glue it around the rim of the new extension (to hide the joins). When the glue has set, glue the smokebox door in position – a very good white-metal casting is available from South Eastern Finecast (from their 'T9' kit).

Next, from card or 1mm-thick Plasticard, manufacture the new cab sides and splasher casings (**Figure 5**), then glue them to the new cab front and each side of the running-plate. Cut out two rectangular pieces of card 65mm by 5mm to form the tops of the splashers; bend each one to shape and glue it in place. At this point in the proceedings the more enterprising loco-builder may wish to construct a cab interior.

Take a 94mm length of 1mm-diameter brass wire (Alan Gibson), and bend it to form the cab rear handrail (**Figure 6**); as it also has to support

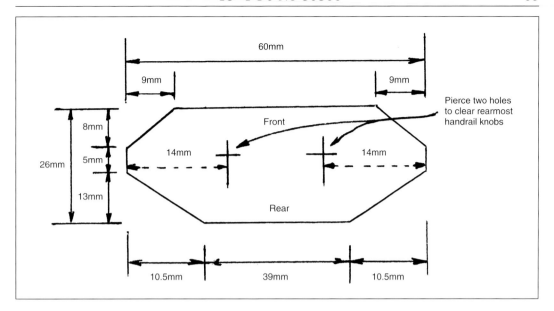

Above Figure 3: Paper cover for firebox

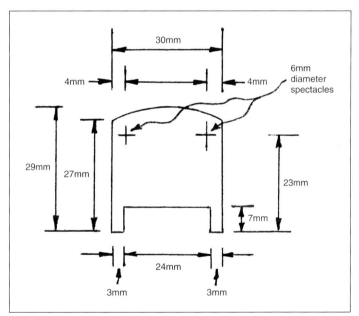

Right Figure 4: New cab front

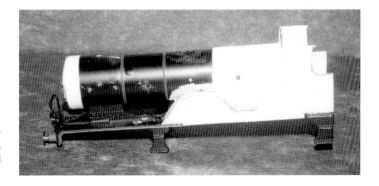

Right The loco body partially constructed. Note the front extension and the new sides, firebox top and patches of filling using Milliput.

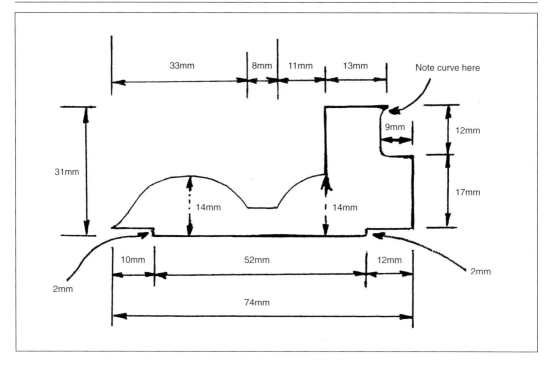

Figure 5: New cab sides and splasher casings

the rear of the cab roof, ensure that the top curve matches the profile of the cab front. Next cut out a rectangle of card 33mm wide by 23mm long to form the cab roof, bend it to shape, and glue it in place. Drill or pierce a 1mm-diameter hole through the top of the firebox 12mm from the cab front, on the centre-line, to take the whistle. At this stage it might be a good idea to paint the splashers, cab front and firebox before fitting the whistle and its associated pipework.

Figure 6: Cab rear handrails

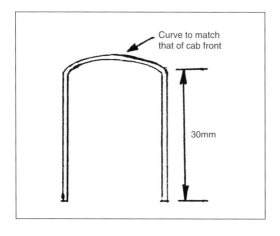

When the paint on the firebox has dried, glue the whistle in position (I re-used the original one from the 2P). Then glue a 12mm length of 1mm-diameter brass wire (Alan Gibson) along the centre-line of the firebox between the cab and the whistle, to represent the pipe that feeds steam to the whistle. Next take two 36mm lengths of 1mm-diameter brass wire, bend them to shape as shown in **Figure 7** and glue them to each side of the firebox as in **Figure 8**. Their top ends should appear to continue into the cab, while their bottom ends should appear to continue into the splasher casings (use photographs as a guide).

In common with most other LSWR designs the cabs of the 'T9s' had three transverse roof-ribs. Manufacture these from 1mm-square microstrip, beginning with two 23mm lengths to form the two sides, then glue them to the outer edges of the cab roof. Then take three 32mm lengths to form the transverse ribs, bend them to shape and glue in place, one along the leading edge of the roof, another along the rear edge, and the third at the exact halfway point (use photographs as a guide).

Next fit the chimney and dome; white-metal

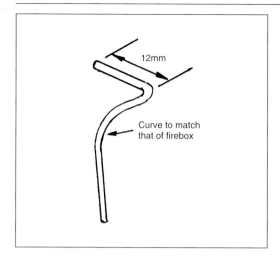

Above Figure 7: Pipes for firebox

Below Figure 8: Firebox pipework

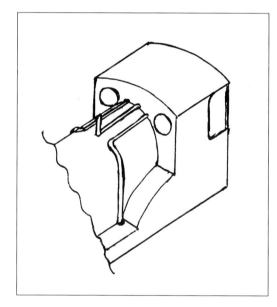

castings for these are available from South Eastern Finecast and are very good quality indeed. The dome goes in the same position as its LMS predecessor, while the chimney needs to be positioned 15mm ahead of the leading boiler-band. Note that the chimney casting comes with a 'capuchon', which may need filing off; most members of the class had these removed in the 1930s, but at least one (No 30119) retained it until the early months of nationalisation.

We now move on to the clack-valves. Markits Ltd produce some very good turned-brass

examples that come with plenty of copper pipework. South Eastern Finecast also produce a very good pair of white-metal castings (from their 'T9' kit), which are already of the correct length and profile and only require painting; I used these on my model. Use photographs as a guide to fitting. With the clack-valves in place we can now fit the boiler handrails. I re-used the original 2P handrail knobs combined with Alan Gibson 0.7mm-diameter brass wire (use photographs as a guide to its profile).

Next fit the lamp-brackets. South-Eastern Finecast and Westward produce very good etched-brass ones. Remember that Southern locos carried six: one at the top of the smokebox, three on the buffer-beam (three holes were drilled for them earlier), and two L-shaped ones on the smokebox door either side of the door-handle (again use photographs as a guide). Refit the vacuum-brake pipe to the front buffer-beam; note that the 'T9s' carried their vacuum-pipes on the opposite side from the 2Ps (consult photographs for guidance). Finally fit a pair of 6mm-diameter brass spectacle surrounds; these are available from Jackson-Evans and Mainly Trains, and they certainly improve the model's appearance.

Stage 3: The loco chassis

The only modification necessary to the loco chassis is the filing or cutting away of the top corners of the metal weight so that the new round-top firebox will fit over it (**Figure 9**).

Figure 9: Removing top corners of chassis weight

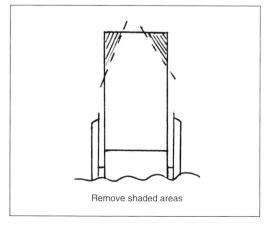

Remove shaded areas

The front and rear of the loco, showing the positions of the lamp-brackets.
The front number plate is made up from Fox transfers.

Stage 4: The tender

As there were no water-troughs on the Southern, the water-dome needs to be removed from the 2P tender body. The easiest way of doing this is to drill it out in stages, commencing with, say, a 2mm drill and going up to 10mm. Clean up the rough edges and cover the resulting hole with a piece of paper 26mm by 13mm. Likewise the control-handle for the water-scoop needs to be removed from the front (left-hand side) of the tender. Next remove the portions of the side-raves aft of the rear coal partition (**Figure 10**). We now need to fashion some coal-rails with which to cover the remains of the side-raves. One option would be to use lengths of 1mm-diameter brass wire, or we could use Slaters Plasticard (sheet 0436 – corrugated iron); I have used this

material in the past for coal-rails and it gives a very good effect. Cut out two pieces (**Figure 11**) and glue them in place over the remains of the tender side-raves.

Now for the rear of the tender, which only has two lamp-brackets, while the 2P should have four, and a Southern loco should have six! While South Eastern Finecast and Westward produce very good etched-brass lamp-brackets, in this instance I preferred to use 2mm lengths of 1mm-square microstrip, which fitted into the confined space quite easily and still gave a pretty good representation of lamp-brackets. Next fit a set of Springside fire-irons to the top of the tender; these make a real difference to the final appearance of the model.

With that job done the model is now ready for painting and transfers. The livery carried in BR days was 'mixed traffic' and the power-

Figure 10: Dissection of tender body

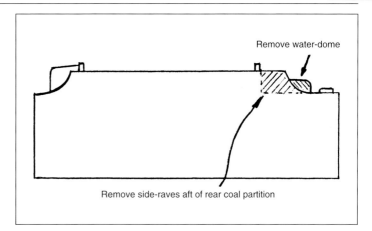

Remove water-dome

Remove side-raves aft of rear coal partition

Figure 11: Manufacture of new side-raves for tender

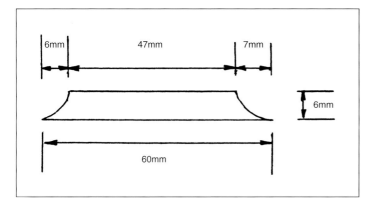

classification was 2P until circa 1956, when they were re-classified 3P. This classification was carried on the cab sides above the fleet number.

So there we have it, another useful addition to any Southern layout, especially one based on the 'Withered Arm'.

Ex-SR '700' 0-6-0 No 30306

In 1897 the LSWR introduced its '700' Class of 0-6-0 freight locomotives. They were designed by Dugald Drummond and a total of 30 locos were built. The design employed a 180psi boiler, two inside cylinders of 19 by 26 inches, and 5ft 1in-diameter driving wheels. They were of quite conventional appearance until being rebuilt (with superheaters) by R. W. Urie from 1921. The fitting of a superheated boiler necessitated the extension of the smokebox, which, together with Urie's passion for fitting stovepipe chimneys, completely transformed the outward appearance of the locos.

As regards performance, they must have been good because all 30 locos survived to become BR property in 1948, and my Autumn 1961 *Locoshed Book* shows 25 of them still surviving. The class finally became extinct with the withdrawal of Nos 30687, 30689 and 30700 off Exmouth Junction in January 1964. So here is yet another long-lived class (more than 60 years) whose members could be seen in London, on the 'Withered Arm', and all points in between. If your layout is set in the South Western Division, one of these locos is a must! (The class history was compiled with the assistance of *Locomotives Illustrated* Part 64 'Pre-grouping Southern 0-6-0s' by P. F. Winding, published by Ian Allan Ltd.)

Items required

Airfix/Dapol/Hornby ex-LMS 4F 0-6-0 loco and tender; detailing parts as described in the text.

Stage 1: The loco body

First remove the LMS-style pipework on the left-hand side of the boiler (it is only a clip-fit so a penknife blade should do the trick). Remove the boiler handrails, then the cab (again this is only a clip-fit so a penknife blade should suffice). Next remove the vacuum brake pipe from the front buffer-beam and retain it for re-use on the new model. Remove the smokebox door (again this is a clip-fit item) and remove the lead weight from inside the boiler; it is held in place by a screw on its underside (retain the weight for re-use on the new model).

With a hacksaw, remove the chimney and dome, and file any residue flush with the boiler. Then, with a craft-knife, first remove the mechanical lubricators from the right-hand running-plate, then the piston tail-rods from the front buffer-beam. Remove the raised central portion of the front buffer-beam. Next, with a hacksaw, remove the top of the Belpaire firebox, then cut a vertical slot in the sides of the firebox 21mm forward from the rear of the footplate; make sure that you leave the rear splashers intact (**Figure 1**). Next, with Milliput or similar, fill in the holes in the body left by the removal of the chimney, dome, boiler-side pipes and mechanical lubricators. Also fill in the recesses in the firebox sides for the rear sandbox fillers.

Now, from card or Plasticard, manufacture a new cab front (**Figure 2**), and try it in place, enlarging the slot in the firebox sides if necessary. When you are satisfied that the cab front is a straight and square fit, replace the lead weight in its original position inside the body (at the same time ensuring that the new cab front also clears the weight). With this done, glue the cab front in position.

Next cut out a rectangle of card 25mm by 19mm to form the new firebox top, bend it to shape and glue in place. From a piece of paper 20mm by 68mm manufacture a cover for the firebox to hide the joins and the 'threepenny-bit

Above What was to become one of the last three surviving '700' Class 0-6-0s, No 30689, is seen at Weybridge on the afternoon of 5 July 1960. *David Holmes*

Below The completed model, with Springside fire-irons and transfers by Fox, SMS and Modelmaster.

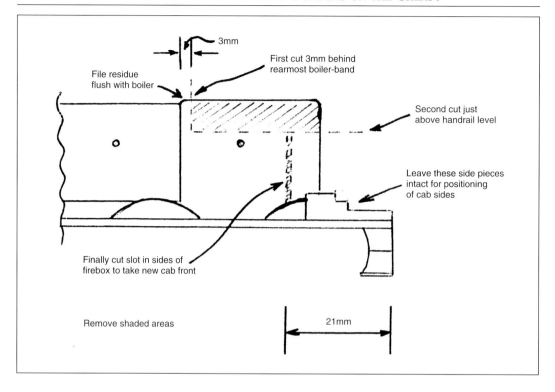

Above Figure 1: Modifications to firebox

Below Figure 2: Manufacture of new cab front with slot for body weight

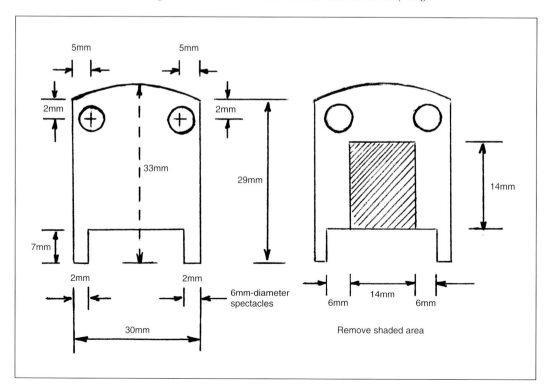

Figure 3: Paper cover for firebox

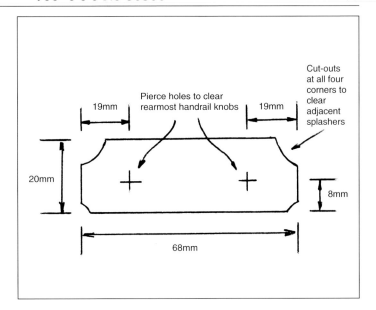

Figure 4: Manufacture of new cab sides

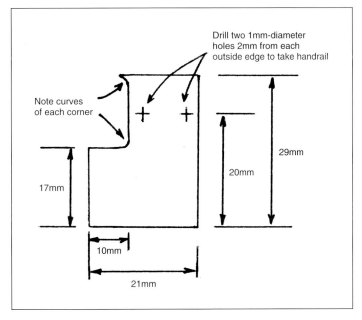

effect' (**Figure 3**), then glue it in place. Next, from card or Plasticard, manufacture new cab sides (**Figure 4**). After fitting the cab-side handrails (I used 0.7mm-diameter wire, produced by Alan Gibson), glue the new cab sides in place. At this point the more enterprising loco-builders may wish to manufacture a new (round) top for the firebox backhead.

From an 85mm length of 0.9mm-diameter brass wire (again supplied by Alan Gibson),

manufacture the cab handrails, which also act as supports for the cab-roof (**Figure 5**), and glue in place at the rear of the cab. The cab roof is manufactured from card 21mm by 31mm, bent to shape and glued in place. Manufacture the roof-ribs from 1mm-square microstrip. Glue a 22mm length along each of the two cant-rails. Then take three 29mm lengths to form the transverse ribs, bend them to shape, and glue them in place, one on each outside edge, and the third across the exact centre of the roof.

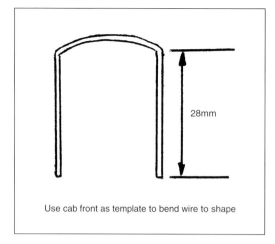

Use cab front as template to bend wire to shape

Above Figure 5: Manufacture of rear cab handrails

Below Figure 6: New cover for valve chests

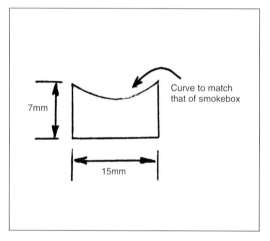

Pierce a hole through the top of the firebox, on the centre-line 8mm from the cab front, to take the whistle. Then drill a 1mm-diameter hole through each side of the boiler 5mm below the level of the handrail and 5mm to the rear of the second handrail knob; these two holes will take the clack-valves.

Manufacture a new valve-chest cover from card (**Figure 6**) and glue it in place at the base of the smokebox front.

The next job is to manufacture, from card or Plasticard, the combined front splashers and sandboxes (**Figure 7**). In order to fit them in place you will need to remove a couple of small lugs (one on each side of the running-plate just in advance of the LMS-style sandbox-fillers). With these lugs out of the way the new fabrications will sit comfortably in place over the original 4F splashers (see photographs as a guide).

We now move on to the smokebox extension. First cut out *two* 22mm-diameter discs of card and glue one to the front of the 4F smokebox. Then cut out a 22mm-diameter disc of 3mm-thick Plasticard or balsa-wood and glue it to the front of the smokebox, and glue the second card disc to the front of the balsa-wood or Plasticard disc. Next cut out a piece of paper 70mm long by 4.5mm wide and glue it around the outside rim of the newly created smokebox extension, to hide the joins.

We now move on to the boiler mountings and other detail castings. South-Eastern Finecast Ltd

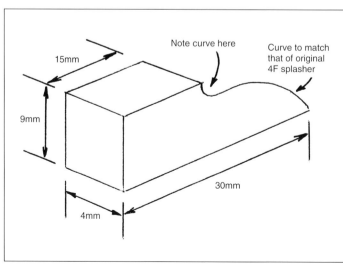

Figure 7: Manufacture of new combined front splashers and sand-boxes

produce a very good model of an LSWR Class 'T9' 4-4-0, which is virtually a 'stretched' '700' Class with a 4-4-0 wheel arrangement. Thus the chimney, dome, smokebox door, clack-valves and whistle from this kit are perfect for our needs. The castings supplied were 'fine and crisp' with little or no 'flash'; the smokebox door has a handle incorporated into the moulding, so that came out of the packet and straight onto the model with no modifications necessary. The 'T9' chimney comes with a 'capuchon', which is soon cut or filed off, and the casting glued to the top of the smokebox with its leading edge in line with the front of the original 4F smokebox. The Drummond dome (with the safety-valves mounted on top) is located in line with the centre of the middle splashers. Fit the whistle in place on the top of the firebox, and check that all three boiler-mounted items are straight and in line. Then fit the clack-valves in place (use photographs as a guide); considering that the South Eastern Finecast product is a white-metal

casting, the associated pipework (which seemed to go on for ever with Southern locos) is very well done indeed and I recommend it. As regards the reversing-rod, I retained the original 4F version, which is very close to that of the '700'.

The next job is to fit the lamp-brackets. Westward produce some very good ones, including the additional SR brackets that go on the sides of the smokebox door (use photographs as a guide). Next refit the original vacuum-pipe to the buffer-beam. Jackson-Evans produce some very good etched circular spectacles for the cab windows – the 6mm-diameter ones are reference number G.61 in the range. Fitting a pair of these certainly improves the appearance of the model.

We now move on to the whistle and its associated pipework. Having already fixed the South Eastern Finecast white-metal casting in place, I used Alan Gibson 1mm-diameter brass wire for the pipework. Cut two 34mm lengths to run from each side of the whistle to the running-plate; bend them to the same profile as the

Front and rear views of the model, showing the position of the SR lamp-brackets.

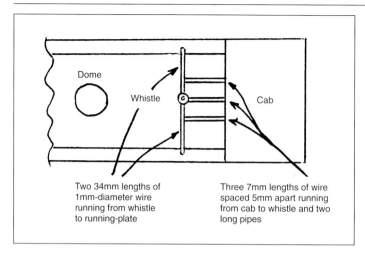

Figure 8: Whistle and associated pipework

firebox and glue in place. Then cut three 7mm lengths to run from the front of the cab to the whistle and the two longer pipes (**Figure 8**).

The next job is the fitting of the handrail. The '700s' had continuous handrails (use photographs as a guide). I used 0.45mm-diameter brass wire supplied by Alan Gibson, and re-used the original 4F handrail knobs, a combination that worked out pretty well. The loco is now complete and ready for painting. The livery carried in BR days was unlined black, and the power classification was 4F until circa 1955 when the locos were downgraded to 3F. Some (but not all) carried the power classification on their cab sides.

Stage 2: The tender body

As there were no water-troughs on the Southern the tender water-dome needs to be removed from the 4F tender. The easiest way of doing this is to drill it out in stages, commencing with, say, a 4mm drill and going up to 10mm. Clean up the rough edges and cover the resulting hole with a piece of paper 26mm by 13mm. Likewise the control-handle for the water-scoop needs to be removed from the front (left-hand side) of the tender. Next remove the portions of the side-raves aft of the rear coal partition (**Figure 9**). We now need to fashion some coal-rails with which to cover the remains of the side raves. One option would be to use lengths of 1mm-diameter brass wire, or we could use Slaters Plasticard sheet 0436 (corrugated iron). I have used this material in the past for coal-rails and it gives a very good effect. Cut out two pieces (**Figure 10**) and glue them in place over the remains of the tender side-raves.

Now for the rear of the tender. It only has two

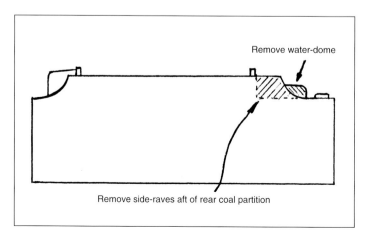

Figure 9: Dissection of tender body

Figure 10: Manufacture of new side-raves for tender

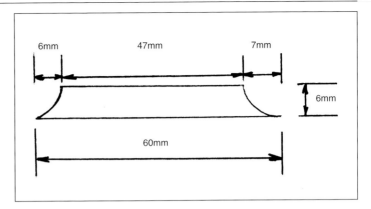

lamp-brackets, while the 4F should have four and a Southern loco should have six! While South Eastern Finecast and Westward produce very good etched-brass lamp-brackets, in this instance I preferred to use 2mm lengths of 1mm-square microstrip, which fitted into the confined space fairly easily and still gave a pretty good representation of lamp-brackets.

With this job done the tender is now ready for paint and transfers, etc, completing a very interesting and useful addition to any South Western Division layout.

Ex-SR 'L' 4-4-0 No 31773

In 1914 the South Eastern & Chatham Railway introduced its Class 'L' 4-4-0 express passenger locomotives. The design is normally credited to Harry S. Wainwright, Chief Mechanical Engineer of the SE&CR from 1899 to 1913, but some sources credit it to Robert Surtees (Wainwright's chief draughtsman). Wainwright retired n 1913, leaving his successor, R. E. L. Maunsell, to 'tidy up' the design and gain authorisation from the board of directors for the construction of 22 locomotives. Tenders for their construction were accepted from Beyer Peacock & Co of Manchester (12 locos) and A. Borsig & Co of Berlin, Germany (10 locos). All 22 were introduced to service in 1914. The design employed 6ft 8in-diameter driving wheels, two inside cylinders, a Belpaire firebox, and a steam-reverser. The class originally worked the SE&CR top-link services (including the Dover boat trains), but by the late 1930s the onset of heavier trains saw them displaced to secondary services by more modern designs.

All 22 locos survived to become BR property in 1948, but electrification and dieselisation saw them displaced from even the most mundane duties. Some were withdrawn (beginning with No 31769 in 1956), while others migrated to the Central Division, and later a few survivors found refuge on the South Western Division, with Eastleigh (71A) and Nine Elms (70A) each receiving small allocations. My 1961 Ian Allan *Locoshed Book* shows four survivors (Nos 31760/31768/31771 and 31780) all allocated to Nine Elms (70A), and these ended their days pottering around the London end of the South Western Division on parcels trains and empty coaching stock workings. The class was finally rendered extinct in 1962 with the condemnation of No 31768.

Items required

Mainline/Dapol/Hornby ex-LMS Class 2P loco and tender; detailing parts as described in the text.

Stage 1: The loco-body

First remove the cab. This is only a 'clip-fit', so a penknife blade should do the job. Then remove the side panels of the leading splashers, the LMS-pattern reversing-rod, the LMS-pattern vacuum-ejector pipes from the side of the smokebox, and both mechanical lubricators. Using a pair of pliers, remove all the boiler handrails, and the handrail knobs from the sides of the smokebox (leave those on the sides of the boiler and firebox in situ). Then, with a hacksaw, remove the chimney and dome, and file the 'stumps' flush with the boiler and smokebox. File away the raised mouldings from the left-hand side of the smokebox (left by the removal of the vacuum-ejector pipe). Remove the whistle with a pair of pliers and set aside for re-use on the new model, then, in order to facilitate the fitting of the new cab front, remove the rear 2mm of the firebox together with part of each rear splasher (**Figure 1**). File away the superheater header and the four prominent protrusions on the top edges of the firebox (washout plugs?). Then file away the centre boiler-band – the 'Ls' had four boiler-bands whereas the 2Ps only had three (again see **Figure 1**).

Next, to facilitate the fitting of the new splasher castings, cut or file back the raised portions of the running-plate to a depth of 1mm (**Figure 2**). Then drill a 1mm-diameter hole through each side of the boiler, in line with and 4mm below the handrail knobs (also **Figure 2**), to take the clack-valves. Next drill a 1mm-

Above 'L' Class 4-4-0 No 31773, the loco being modelled, at Tonbridge on 3 August 1958. *David Holmes*

Below The completed model of No 31773, with transfers by SMS, Fox and Modelmaster. Note the yellow spot beneath the fleet number denoting the fitting of the BR water-softening equipment.

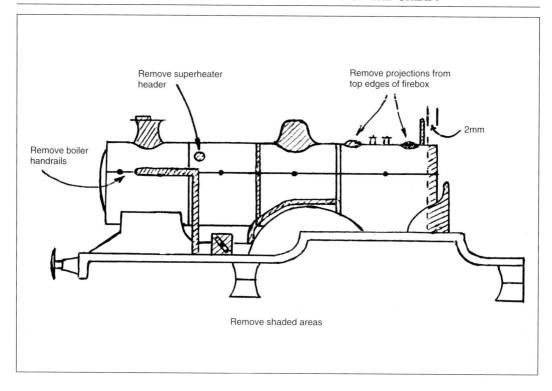

Figure 1: Modifications to loco body

Figure 2: Further modifications to loco body

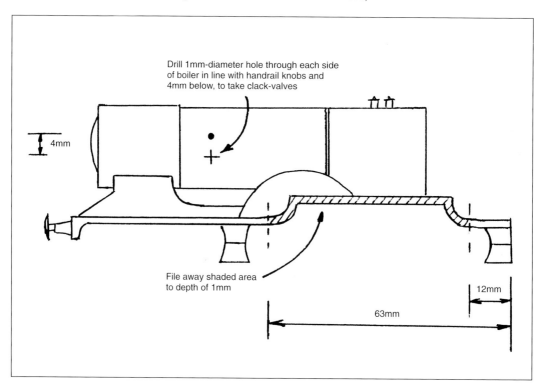

Figure 3: Wrappers for smokebox

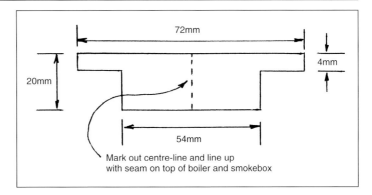

Figure 4: New cab front

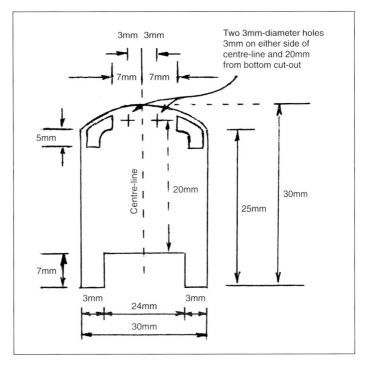

diameter hole through the top of the firebox 1mm behind the rear safety-valve, on the centre-line, to take the whistle. Also drill three 1mm-diameter holes through the top edge of the buffer-beam, to take the lamp-brackets, one directly above the coupling, and the other two 4mm in from each outside edge. The removal of the reversing-rod will have left a 'trough' above the leading splasher on the left-hand side of the loco, so fill this with Milliput or similar and, when set, file any surplus flush with emery-cloth.

Manufacture two new boiler-bands from 1mm-wide strips of paper, Glue one of the strips 13mm to the rear of the leading boiler-band, and the second 13mm ahead of the front of the

firebox. With this done you should have four boiler-bands on the boiler with a 13mm gap between each one. We now turn our attention to the smokebox, the diameter of which needs to be increased by 2mm (6 inches on the real thing). To achieve this, cut out a piece of 1mm-thick card (**Figure 3**) and glue it in place wrapped around the outside of the smokebox. Then cut out a piece of paper to the same dimensions and glue it over the card 'wrapper' to hide the 'threepenny-bit effect'. The smokebox is now a scale 6 inches wider. Next manufacture a new cab front (**Figure 4**) and glue it to the rear of the firebox, ensuring that the cut out at the bottom clears the rear pair of driving wheels.

We now move on to the most complicated part of this conversion, the manufacture of the new sides for the cab and splashers. This involves an attempted replication of Mr Wainwright's (or Mr Surtees's) reverse curve, while at the same time ensuring that they fit over the existing splashers and firebox of the Hornby 2P. What I arrived at for my model is shown in **Figure 5**. Manufacture the sides from 1mm-thick card or Plasticard, then drill two 1mm-diameter holes through each cab side (**Figure 6**) to take the cab-side handrails; use photographs as a guide. Thread a short length of 0.7mm-diameter brass wire (available from Alan Gibson) through the

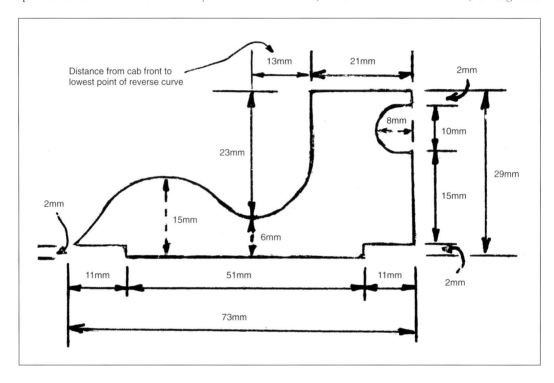

Above Figure 5: New sides for cab and splashers

Below The loco body under construction. Note the new boiler-bands and the smokebox wrapper.

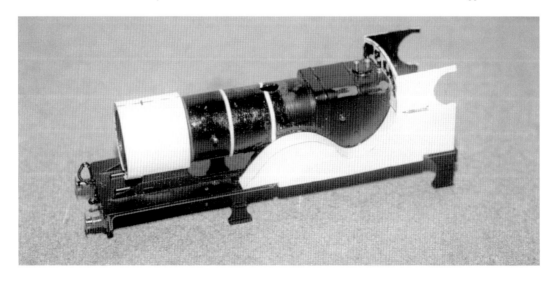

holes on each cab side and bend over the ends on the inside with a pair of pliers. With this done the sides can be glued in place.

Next cut out two lengths of thin card 5mm wide by 66mm long to form the tops of the splashers. Glue them in place along the tops of the splashers with their rear ends fixed to the cab front (again use photographs as a guide).

Manufacture the cab rear handrails from 1mm-diameter brass wire (also available from Alan Gibson) as shown in **Figure 7**, and glue it to the rear edges of the cab sides. Next cut out a rectangle of card 35mm wide by 23mm long to form the cab roof. Bend it to shape and glue it in place. At this point it would be a good idea to paint the loco body and, when the paint has dried, apply the boiler-band transfers.

We now move on to the boiler-mounted items. For the chimney and dome I used a couple of white-metal castings from South Eastern Finecast (from their SR Maunsell Class 'Q' loco kit). These are very close to the required profiles and very good-quality castings. The chimney and dome go in the same positions as their LMS predecessors. For the whistle re-use the one from the 2P inserted into the hole drilled earlier. Next glue the clack-valves in position, again using the holes drilled earlier; suitable white-metal castings are available from South Eastern Finecast (from their SR Class 'D' or 'Q' loco kits). Markits Ltd also produce a pair of SR clack-valves made from turned brass and copper, which are also of very good quality, but in order to assemble them you need an extra pair of hands and the eyesight of a hawk! Also, at the time of writing, plastic mouldings for the Hornby 'Schools' clack-valves are available from Modelspares, and East Kent Models of Whitstable.

We now turn our attention to the steam-reverser. I am afraid I do not know of any manufacturer that produces a casting in OO gauge for one of these; however, they were so similar in outward appearance to a Westinghouse pump that a casting for one of these would be an ideal substitute; white-metal castings are available from many sources, including South Eastern Finecast, Dave Alexander, Jackson-Evans, Westward Models and Craftsman Models. Also, at the time of

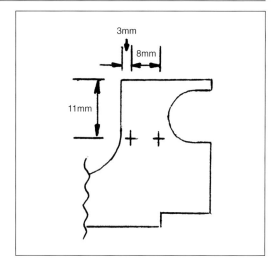

Above Figure 6: Cab-side handrails

Below Figure 7: Cab rear handrails

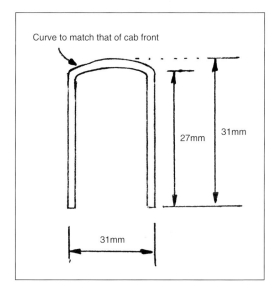

writing a plastic moulding for a Westinghouse pump (from the Hornby 'E2') is also available from East Kent Models of Whitstable. Once you have obtained your Westinghouse pump, glue it to the right-hand side of the loco, in an upright position with its base on the running-plate, and in line with the second boiler-band (again use photographs as a guide).

Now a word or two about mechanical lubricators. Some members of the class carried a Wakefield mechanical lubricator on the left-hand running-plate between the first boiler-band and the feed-pipe to the clack-valve (again work from a photograph of the loco you wish to model). Suitable white-metal castings are available from Dave Alexander, Westward Models, Dave Bradwell and Craftsman Models.

Next fit the boiler handrails. On the right-hand side re-use the original from the 2P, and use a length of 0.7mm-diameter brass wire (available from Alan Gibson) for the left-hand side. Use the same size wire for the boiler-side piping and cable-runs: (1) along the right-hand side from the cab front to the reverser (steam supply pipe to the reverser); (2) on the right-hand side from the cab front to the rear edge of the leading splasher (steam supply to the cylinder drain-cocks); and (3) on the left-hand side, running from the cab front, over the splashers and dipping down to disappear out of sight under the smokebox saddle (again use photographs as a guide).

Next cut out a piece of card or Plasticard 4mm square, to form the fireman's step on which he would stand to clean out the smokebox. Glue it to the bottom edge of the smokebox front astride the vertical centre-line. Now fit the front lamp-brackets: three on the buffer-beam, utilising the holes drilled earlier through the top of the buffer-beam, and two on the outside edges of the smokebox front (use photographs as a guide). As regards the top lamp-bracket, the original from the 2P is in the correct position for the SR Class 'L' in BR days. Sets of etched-brass lamp-brackets are available from Westward Models and South Eastern Finecast.

Stage 2: The tender body

All members of Class 'L' were equipped with 3,450-gallon tenders with a wheelbase of 13ft 0in, which is the same as the tenders coupled to the LMS 2Ps. South Eastern Finecast produce a kit for one of these SE&CR tenders (from their Class 'D' kit). This has a white-metal body that could be adapted to fit over the mechanism of the 2P tender. However, failing this, the Mainline/Dapol/Hornby 2P tender body can be rebuilt into something resembling one of the SE&CR examples.

First remove the water-dome. I found that the easiest way to do this was to drill it out, starting with a 2mm-diameter drill and going up in stages

Front and rear views of the model showing the additional lamp-brackets. Those on the front are by Westward, with transfers by SMS, while on the rear of the tender they are formed of pieces of 1mm-square microstrip.

to 10mm; doing it in stages guards against cracking/splitting of the surrounding plastic. With this done, remove the water-scoop control-handle (the handle on the right-hand side of the tender footplate – there were no water-troughs on the Southern). Then, with a craft-knife, remove the side-raves to the rear of the coal-space (**Figure 8**). Also file or cut away the beading on the top edge of the tender rear (again see **Figure 8**). With all of this done we can start the reassembly. Cover the hole left by the removal of the water-dome with a piece of paper or thin card. Manufacture the new side-raves

from 1mm-thick Plasticard (**Figure 9**) and glue them to the tender body with their top and leading edges in line with those of the tender body, thus giving the impression of a stepped tender top.

The rear ends of the Wainwright SE&CR tenders had flared tops. In order to simulate this, take two 80mm lengths of 1mm-square microstrip and glue them to the sides of the tender body directly below the newly fitted side-raves. Ensure that their top edges are level with those of the tender rear (around the water-space). Then take a 31mm length of 1mm-square

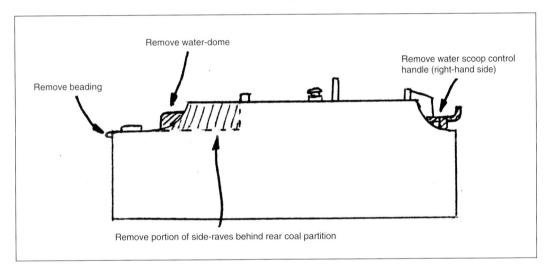

Figure 8: Dissection of tender body

The completed tender body prior to painting.

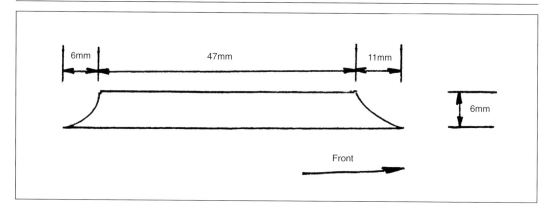

Figure 9: New side-raves for tender

microstrip and glue it across the rear of the tender with its top edge level with that of the tender rear. We now turn our attention to the tender lamp-brackets; SR locos had six, 'normal' locos four, and the Hornby 2P only two! Manufacture the four missing lamp-brackets from 2mm lengths of 1mm-square microstrip and glue them in the required positions (use photographs as a guide).

The model is now ready for paint and transfers. The livery carried in BR days was 'mixed traffic', and the power classification was 2P (upgraded to 3P from 1956), and all locos carried this above their fleet numbers on the cab sides. Most locos also carried a yellow spot below the fleet number denoting that they were fitted with the BR water-softening system (as carried by some of the 'Pacifics').

Ex-SR 'E5X' 0-6-2T No 32401

In 1911 Douglas Earl Marsh (CME of the LB&SCR) rebuilt four members of Class 'E5' (Nos 401, 570, 576 and 586) with larger 5ft 0in-diameter boilers, as fitted to his recently introduced 'C3' Class of 0-6-0 tender engines. The four rebuilt locomotives became Class 'E5X' (the 'X' suffix denoting a rebuild). One of the four locos (No 401) received a double-domed boiler (the second dome housed an LMS/GWR-pattern top-feed). Unfortunately what little improvement was gained by fitting the larger boiler was cancelled out by an increase in fuel consumption.

After the Grouping of 1923 all of the ex-LB&SCR-owned locomotives had their running numbers increased by 2000. Another change brought about by the Grouping was the transferring of maintenance of some ex-LB&SCR locos (including the 'E5Xs') to the former South Eastern Railway's workshops at Ashford (Kent). Between the Grouping and the outbreak of war in 1939 Ashford carried out further modifications – the cylinders were reduced in diameter, and dual brakes (vacuum and Westinghouse) and SER-pattern injectors were fitted – and two of the locos (Nos 2401 and 2576) were fitted with SER Wainwright-pattern smokebox doors.

All four locos survived to become BR property in 1948, and all were withdrawn off Brighton shed (75A) during the 1950s, No 32401 in July 1954, No 32570 in January 1956, No 32576 in July 1955, and No 32586 in March 1955.

Although there were only four locos in the class, and they only ventured outside Central Division territory when visiting Ashford for repairs/overhaul, one of them (especially the double-domed example) would be something unusual for a Southern-based layout.

Items required

Hornby LNER Class 'N2' 0-6-2T; detailing parts as described in the text. (The Dapol and Mainline versions of the 'N2' could also be used for this conversion but as their mechanisms are larger the design of the new cab would need to be altered accordingly.)

Stage 1: Dissecting the body

First separate the body from the chassis; they are held together by a screw underneath the smokebox and two lugs at the rear of the bunker. Next remove the cab; this is only a 'clip-fit' (with a lug fitting under the firebox and another fitting under the top of the coal space), so a penknife blade should do the trick. Then remove the tank vents, and the safety-valves. Remove the whistle and retain it for re-use, and remove the condensing pipes from both sides of the locomotive; again, a penknife blade should lift them off (**Figure 1**). Next remove the smokebox door, which should come away with a push from behind with a screwdriver. Remove the handrails from the tops of the tanks, again using a penknife blade, then, with a hacksaw, remove the dome, chimney and snifting-valve. File any residue flush with the top of the boiler and smokebox.

We now come to the most difficult part of this conversion – the removal of the front sandboxes. This is best carried out with a craft-knife, and it is essential that you carefully cut around the outside curve of the splasher to leave its profile intact.

Above Double-domed 'E5X' 0-6-2T No 32401 was withdrawn in July 1954, and is seen here at Ashford Works in September of that year. *Frank Hornby*

Below The completed model. Although the spacing of the driving wheels is incorrect, I am pleased with the result! The transfers are a mixture of SMS, Fox and Modelmaster.

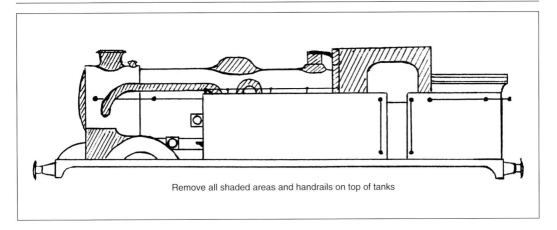

Remove all shaded areas and handrails on top of tanks

Figure 1: Modifications to 'N2' body

Stage 2: Reassembling the body

First drill three 1mm-diameter holes through the front of the running-plate, 2mm from its leading edge, to take the lamp-brackets. The centre hole needs to be in line with the coupling-hook, while the two outer holes need to be 4mm in from the outside edges. Next, from card or thin Plasticard, manufacture a pair of new sides for the smokebox saddle (**Figure 2**), and glue them in place. Cut out two pieces of paper 4mm wide by 30mm long to form the new tops for the splashers. Glue the paper strips in place with PVA adhesive – this allows plenty of slide for making last-minute adjustments, and it soaks into the paper and sets rock-hard!

Using Milliput or similar, fill in the holes in

the smokebox sides and the tops of the tanks left by the removal of the condensing pipes and handrails. Also fill in the holes left by the removal of the safety-valves, whistle and chimney. When the filler has set, file flush with emery-cloth. Next cut out two rectangular pieces of 80 thou (2mm-thick) Plasticard 44mm by 20mm to form the new tank sides. With a file or emery-cloth, round off the top outside edges (use photographs as a guide). With this done, glue the new sides over the existing sides with their leading edges in line. When the glue has set, work some filler into the joins of the leading edges.

We now move on to the clack-valves. The tops of the 'E5X' clack-valves were level with the boiler handrails, which curved around them. On this model I decided to invoke a bit of 'modeller's licence' and left the original boiler handrails undisturbed. I drilled a 1mm-diameter hole through each side of the boiler 3mm below the handrail and 9mm from the leading edge of each tank, and used a pair of castings from the old Nu-Cast range; however, their products are getting somewhat scarce nowadays, but alternative sources are Craftsman Models, South Eastern Finecast and even Hornby (at the time of writing plastic mouldings from the Hornby 'Schools' are available form East Kent Models, and Modelspares).

As mentioned earlier, Nos 32401 and 32576 were fitted with a South Eastern Railway Wainwright-pattern smokebox door, while 32570 and 32586 retained their original Marsh-

Figure 2: New sides for smokebox saddle

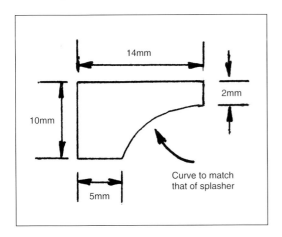

14mm

2mm

10mm

5mm

Curve to match that of splasher

pattern doors. White-metal castings for the Wainwright smokebox door are available from South Eastern Finecast (from their SE&CR Class 'D' kit), while the smokebox door from a Hornby 'Saint' or '28xx' would be very close to the Marsh-pattern door. In order to fit the new smokebox door, manufacture a new front for the smokebox from card or Plasticard (**Figure 3**). Glue the new door to the centre of the new smokebox front, then glue the assembly to the front of the smokebox. While the Hornby smokebox doors have door handles as part of the moulding, the castings from South Eastern Finecast will need a Markits door handle, and they come with a hole drilled in the centre for fitting it. Finally glue the top lamp-bracket to the top of the new smokebox front (again see **Figure 3**).

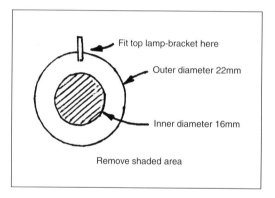

Figure 3: New smokebox front

We can now move on to the lamp-brackets on the buffer-beam. Both Westward and South Eastern Finecast manufacture very good etched-brass lamp-brackets, and on this model I used the Westward variety. Fit the centre bracket first, then fit the two outside ones; the LB&SCR pattern were long enough to hold two discs (one above the other) so they need to be at least 8mm high! The packs of Westward lamp-brackets include some long brass strips that can be cut to the required length (ideal for this job!).

We now turn our attention to the boiler mountings. The 'E5Xs' had Ramsbottom safety-valves enclosed in a metal casing (as with all other Marsh creations), and South Eastern Finecast produce a very good white-metal casting for one of these (from their 'E2' kit). To fit this drill a 3mm-diameter hole through the top of the firebox on the centre-line, 6mm from its rear edge (**Figure 4**). Then drill a 1mm-diameter hole to take the whistle (I re-used the one from the 'N2'), 3mm from the rear edge of the firebox, 5mm to the right of the centre-line (again see **Figure 4**).

As regards the chimney, the nearest I could find to the required pattern was a white-metal casting for a Maunsell Class 'Q' chimney produced by South Eastern Finecast, which is reasonably close to what we want and is the correct height. The chimney needs to be positioned with its centre 10mm from the front of the smokebox. Likewise, the dome for the

The front of the model: note the Wainwright-pattern smokebox door and the LB&SCR-pattern lamp-brackets.

Figure 4: Location of whistle and safety-valves

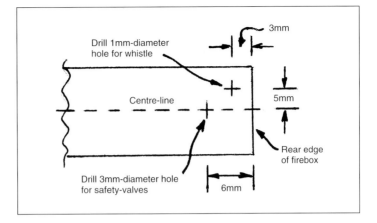

Maunsell Class ‘Q’ from South Eastern Finecast is close to the required pattern and height. If you are modelling one of the single-domed locos the dome goes in the same position as its LNER predecessor. If modelling No 32401, the rear dome goes in the same position as that of the ‘N2’, and the centre of the leading dome needs to be 14mm to the rear of the first boiler-band (again use photographs as a guide).

We now move on to the construction of the new cab. First, from thin card, cut out a rectangular piece 32mm by 6mm and glue it across the tops of the cab side-sheets (**Figure 5**). Then cut out two rectangular pieces 8mm by 6mm and glue them to the tops of the rear cab side-sheets (again see **Figure 5**). Next manufacture a new cab front from card or Plasticard (**Figure 6**), a new cab rear (**Figure 7**), and a pair of new cab sides (**Figure 8**).

Figure 5: Supports for new cab

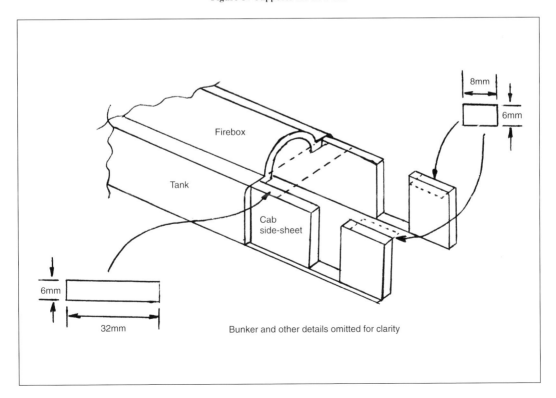

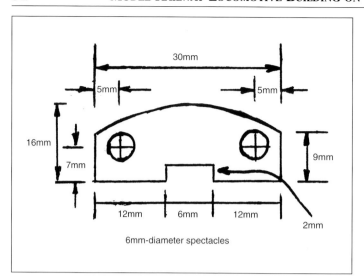

Figure 6: New cab front

6mm-diameter spectacles

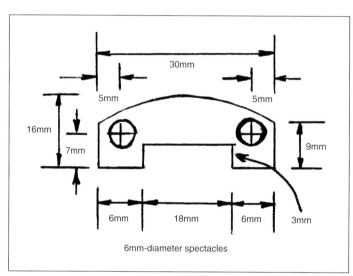

Figure 7: New cab rear

6mm-diameter spectacles

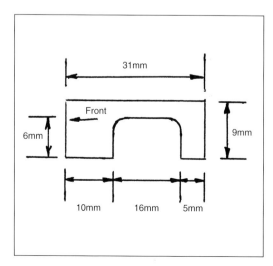

Left Figure 8: New cab sides

Below Figure 9: Vacuum-ejector pipe

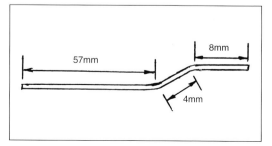

The rear spectacles need to be fitted with coal-guards. Mainly Trains produce a set of etched-brass cab spectacles that includes the type (and size) that we need (item number MT.226 in their catalogue). Glue the spectacles in place, then glue the cab front in place, followed by the cab rear, then the two sides. When the glue has set, paint the inside of the cab. Next cut out a rectangle of card 36mm wide by 32mm long to form the cab roof, bend it to shape and glue in place. Take a 70mm length of 1mm-diameter brass wire (Alan Gibson) and bend it to form the vacuum-ejector pipe (**Figure 9**). Glue it in place on the left-hand side of the boiler – the pipe should enter the cab just below the left-hand spectacle (use photographs as a guide).

Next manufacture the roof rain-strips from 1mm-diameter brass wire (also available from Alan Gibson). Cut two 30mm lengths and glue one to each side of the roof 2mm in from the outside edge. Then glue a couple of extra lamp-brackets to the rear of the bunker. Note that the LB&SCR radial tanks had the rear lamp-brackets arranged in the conventional SR manner. Both South Eastern Finecast and Westward produce very good etched-brass lamp-brackets, which I highly recommend. Next glue a set of fire-irons to the top of the right-hand tank; Springside Models produce a set of white-metal castings for these (item number 61 in their range).

Fit a Westinghouse pump to the right-hand cab side-sheets (use a photograph as a guide to its positioning). Castings for these are available from many sources including Alan Gibson, Dave Alexander, Jackson-Evans, Mainly Trains, South Eastern Finecast and Westward. Fit an extra brake-pipe to each buffer-beam (the 'E5Xs' were dual-braked) – the Romford brass brake-pipes are particularly good. Your model is now ready for painting and transfers; the livery carried in BR days was 'mixed traffic'. Note that all four members of the class were withdrawn before the introduction of the 'Ferret and Dartboard' crest, and the BR power classification was 2MT.

Ex-LMS 7F 'Austin Seven' 0-8-0 No 49508

In 1929 the LMS introduced a new design of 0-8-0 freight locomotives. They had 4ft 8½in-diameter driving wheels, and were designed by Sir Henry Fowler. At the time of their introduction to service 'car-driving for the masses' was just taking off, with the emergence of very cheap cars, one of which was the Austin Seven, and as these locos were in the Class 7 category they quickly earned the nickname 'Austin Sevens'. A total of 175 examples were built, the last three of which were fitted experimentally with ACFI feed-water heaters (as fitted to the LNER 'B12s'), although this equipment was removed well before nationalisation. All the locos were coupled to Fowler 3,500-gallon tenders; some had vents fitted at the rear beside the dome, others had them fitted amidships in the coal space. Some of the tenders had coal-rails, but the majority did not.

All members of the class survived to become BR property in 1948. They could originally be seen on all parts of the LMS system, and also worked inter-regional freights on to other companies', later Regions', metals. None of the class were fitted with vacuum-brakes, which put them at a disadvantage when fully fitted freight trains were introduced. Consequently, with the introduction of the Stanier 8Fs they were quickly displaced from top-link duties. In the immediate post-war years all 175 members of the class were concentrated on ex-L&YR sheds to enable the mass withdrawal of the ex-L&YR 6F and 7F locomotives. Their supremacy on L&YR metals did not last long, however, for with the purchase of the 'WD' 2-8-0s after nationalisation they began to disappear. Withdrawals began in 1949 and continued remorselessly until the class was rendered extinct in January 1962 with the withdrawal of No 49508.

Items required

Hornby 'Patriot' loco body; Hornby 8F or '28xx' (Margate-built) loco chassis; Hornby 'Patriot' tender chassis and power unit; 4F cab (either Hornby or castings from South Eastern Finecast); detailing parts as described in the text.

Stage 1: The loco chassis

First remove the cylinders, motion and 'firebox glow' assembly, then, with a hacksaw, cut away the body fixing lugs from the rear end of the chassis block (**Figure 1**). Next cut or file away the raised portion of the chassis block (used for the location of the 'firebox glow' assembly, then cut away the front 11mm of the chassis block (again see **Figure 1**). Finally file off the Hornby parts reference number ('S.4535.').

Next manufacture a front coupling from thin brass sheet and 1mm-diameter brass wire (**Figure 2**), and fix it to the chassis between the block and the underframe, utilising the two metal lugs on the underside of the block (used for holding the 8F or '28xx' front bogie in place). From a sheet of 80 thou (2mm-thick) Plasticard, cut out a rectangle 124mm by 32mm to form the running-plate, then drill holes in it as shown in **Figure 3**.

Next cut out a piece of 80 thou (2mm-thick) Plasticard 11mm square, and drill a 2mm-diameter hole through its centre; this will form a packing piece for the front cut-away formerly occupied by the 8F and '28xx' cylinder block. Glue the packing piece into the cylinder cut-away and, when the glue has dried, fix the running-plate to the chassis block with two 10BA self-tapping screws.

Next, from 80 thou Plasticard, cut out a

Above 'Austin Seven' 0-8-0 No 49505 at Horwich Works on 22 October 1960. *David Holmes*

Below The completed model. The front sandboxes and mechanical lubricators have been left unpainted so they would show up for the camera! Note also the front coupling, copper pipework and tender fire-irons.

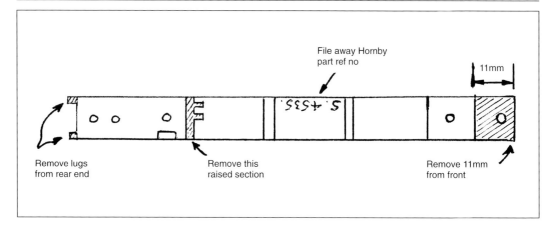

Above Figure 1: Modifications to loco chassis

Below Figure 2: Manufacture of new front coupling

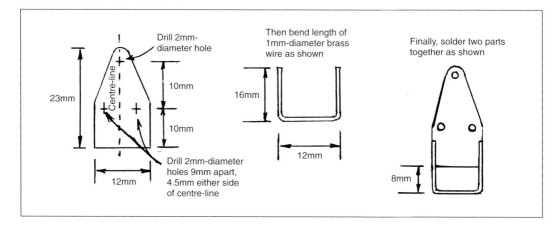

Below Figure 3: New running-plate

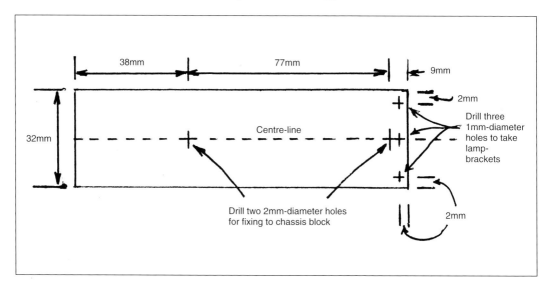

The completed chassis, showing the front coupling, front sandboxes, steps and copper pipework.

rectangle 32mm by 7mm to form the rear drag-beam, and glue it to the rear edges of the running-plate and chassis block.

We now move on to the front buffer-beam, which, because of the high running-plate, needs to be 10mm deep. From a sheet of 2mm-thick Plasticard, cut out a rectangle 32mm by 10mm, and from a sheet of 1mm-thick Plasticard cut out a rectangle 32mm by 5mm. On my model I chose to use Slaters sprung buffers (item number 4903 in their range, 'LMS Standard 16in diameter head'); they are of very high quality and I recommend them. In order to fit the buffers I had to drill 2mm diameter holes through the two pieces of Plasticard (**Figure 4**). I then glued the two buffers to the smaller of the two pieces of Plasticard and, when the glue had set, I painted this part of the buffer-beam red. That done, I painted the larger piece of Plasticard black and, once the paint had dried, I glued the two pieces of Plasticard together with their bottom edges level. When the glue had set I glued the assembled buffer-beam to the front of the chassis with its top edge *underneath* the leading edge of the running-plate. When the glue has set a coupling-hook can be inserted through the centre hole; I used a plastic moulding left over from an Airfix kit, but very good etched brass

coupling-hooks are available (at the time of writing) from Mainly Trains; other possible sources are Markits Ltd and W&T Manufacturing Ltd.

We now turn our attention to the loco-steps. Because of the high running-plate, the steps on the 'Austin Sevens' were higher than most other locos, having three treads instead of the usual two. On my model I adapted a set of white-metal castings from Jackson-Evans (reference M.293 in their range 'Steps for LMS 4-6-0s'). Beginning with the cab steps, I first glued two pieces of balsa-wood 10mm long, 4mm thick and 4mm wide directly underneath the cab floor on each side of the loco. Then I glued onto each piece of balsa-wood a piece of card 10mm by 6mm to form a top step, giving a 2mm overhang. I then glued the pair of rear steps to the underside of each assembly – a bit fiddly, but it worked! For the front steps I cut out two pieces of thin brass 12mm by 4mm and bent them into 'L' shapes with the base of each 'L' 2mm in length. I then glued them to the Jackson-Evans front steps as shown in **Figure 5**. With this done, I glued the two assemblies to the underside of the running-plate 35mm from the leading edge of the front buffer-beam.

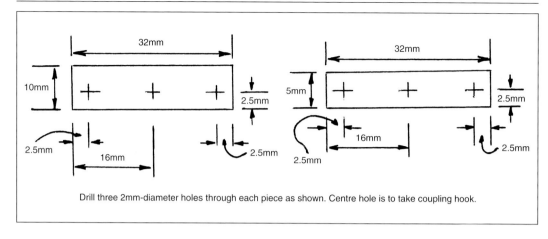

Drill three 2mm-diameter holes through each piece as shown. Centre hole is to take coupling hook.

Figure 4: Construction of front buffer-beam

Next, from a length of 1mm-diameter brass wire, fabricate the injector-pipe for the right-hand side of the loco (**Figure 6**). Give it a coat of Humbrol copper paint (item No 12 in their range) and glue it to the underside of the right-hand running-plate with its rear end glued behind the rear steps (use photographs as a guide). At this point in the proceedings it would be a good idea to fit the lamp-brackets into the three holes that were drilled earlier through the front of the running-plate; etched-brass lamp-brackets are available from South Eastern Finecast and Westward.

Finally, a word or two about the front

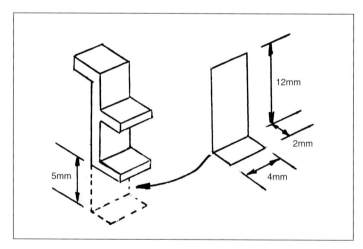

Figure 5: Modifications to front steps

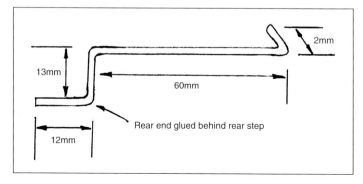

Figure 6: Right-hand injector pipe

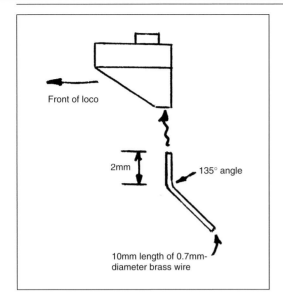

Figure 7: Front sand-boxes

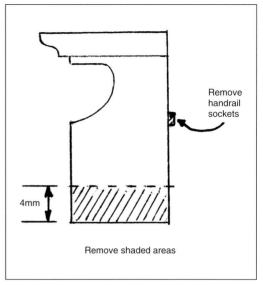

Figure 8: Modifications to 4F cab

Figure 9: New front for cab (Hornby cab only)

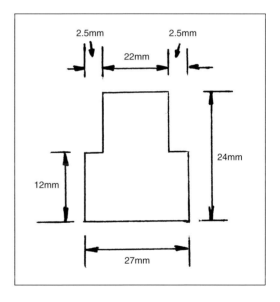

sandboxes. The 'Austin Sevens' had large frame-mounted sandboxes positioned between the buffer-beam and the leading driving wheels. The closest I could find to the required pattern is manufactured by Jackson-Evans (item number W95 in their range – 'GW County Sandboxes'). The castings are of very good quality and come with small holes drilled in the bottom to take a piece of wire to represent the sand delivery pipe. On my model I used two 10mm lengths of 0.7mm-diameter brass wire (from Alan Gibson) and bent them to shape as shown in **Figure 7**. I glued each wire into the small hole in the base of each casting, then glued the assemblies to the sides of the chassis block with their leading edges 20mm from the leading axle.

Stage 2: The loco body

For the construction of this model I used a Hornby 4F cab (left over from a previous conversion). However, if you do not happen to have a 4F cab lying around you could obtain the necessary parts to construct one from South Eastern Finecast (from their 4F kit). If you are using the Hornby plastic moulding you will need to remove the handrail sockets from the cab front (**Figure 8**) and the bottom 4mm from the cab side-sheets (also **Figure 8**). Then manufacture a new cab front from card or

Plasticard (**Figure 9**) and glue it to the inside of the cab.

If you are using the white-metal castings from South Eastern Finecast you will find that the cab sides come with part of the running-plate attached to them; these portions of running-plate will have to be removed with a hacksaw. With this done, remove 4mm from each cab side, and also remove the same amount from the cab front. Clean up the sawn edges with a file or emery-cloth and check for a clean and square fit. When you are satisfied, glue together the cab assembly, ensuring that the base of the cab (the front and two sides) is level.

At this point in the proceedings it would be a good idea to fit the boiler backhead. South Eastern Finecast produce a very good white-metal casting for one of these (again from their 4F loco kit). Also at this stage paint the inside of the cab. When the paint has dried manufacture the two rear handrails from 26mm lengths of 0.7mm-diameter brass wire (available from Alan Gibson), and glue them in place. The cab assembly can now be glued to the rear of the running-plate. Having studied a number of photographs there needs to be a 1mm gap between the rear of the cab and the loco drag-beam. When the glue has set the more enterprising loco-builder may wish to add further detail to the cab interior; South Eastern Finecast produce very good white-metal castings for cab seats and a screw reverser (again from their 4F loco kit).

With the cab glued in place we can now move on to the dissection of the Hornby 'Patriot' loco body. First remove the boiler handrails and the safety-valves and retain them for re-use on the new model. Then remove the chimney and file any residue flush. Next make a vertical hacksaw cut through the firebox immediately in front of the rear-most boiler-band (**Figure 10**), and a horizontal hacksaw cut through the loco body at running-plate level. After removal of the running-plate remove the remains of the splashers, sandboxes, oilboxes, sand-fillers and mechanical lubricators. With a craft-knife, remove the vacuum-ejector and its associated pipework. Next, in order to shorten the smokebox by 6mm, make two vertical hacksaw cuts through the smokebox 6mm apart, 14mm from the leading edge of the smokebox (again see **Figure 10**).

The 'Patriot' safety-valves have a raised base. File this flush with the top of the firebox, then fill in the rearmost of the two holes with Milliput or similar. Next drill a 1mm-diameter hole through the top of the firebox, on the centre-line 3mm from its rear edge, to take the whistle, and a 2mm-diameter hole, also on the centre-line 13mm from its rear edge, to take the leading safety-valve. Next drill a 2mm-diameter hole

Figure 10: Modifications to 'Patriot' loco body

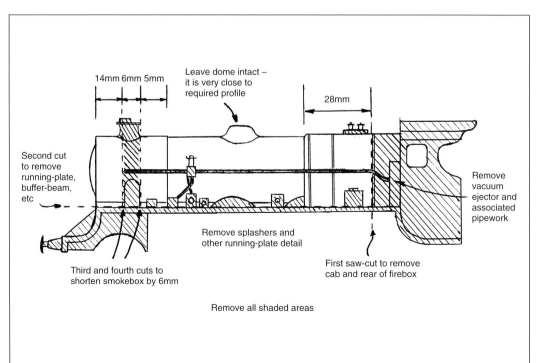

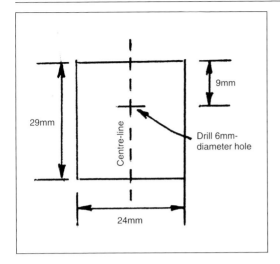

Figure 11: New base for firebox

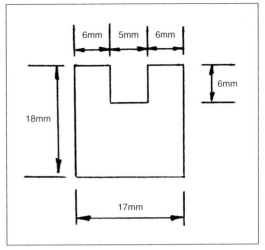

Figure 12: New base for smokebox

Figure 13: New front frames

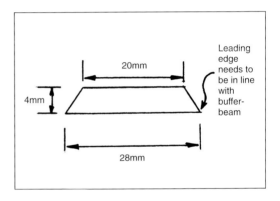

through the top of the smokebox 8mm from its leading edge, to fit the chimney.

Glue the front portion of the smokebox to the rest of the boiler, ensuring that the two parts are straight and square (reinforce the joins with pieces of paper glued to the inside). Next glue the chimney in place; a very good casting is available from Alan Gibson (part number 4M7478 in his range).

From 1mm-thick Plasticard, make new bases for the firebox (**Figure 11**) and smokebox (**Figure 12**). Glue the new firebox base to the bottom of the firebox (the hole is intended to fit over the running-plate fixing-screw and should be nearer to the front of the loco). Do the same with the smokebox base; again, the cut-out should be at the front to clear the front fixing-screw.

When the glue has set use Milliput or similar to fill in the gaps in the smokebox joins, any gaps left in the base of the firebox and smokebox, the holes in the sides of the firebox (caused by the removal of the rear sandboxes), and the holes on either side of the smokebox directly in line with the chimney (previously used for locating the 'Patriot' smoke-deflectors). When the filler has set, file flush with emery-cloth. From card or Plasticard manufacture the new front frames (**Figure 13**), and glue them to the sides of the smokebox saddle, with their leading edges in line with the buffer-beam.

Now that we have the front frames in place we can turn our attention to the small steam-pipes that came out of the smokebox sides and disappeared through the running-plate (I assume they carried steam to the front sandboxes) – refer to photographs. First drill a 1mm-diameter hole through each side of the smokebox 6mm from its leading edge and 6mm above the base of the front frames. Take a length of 0.9mm-diameter brass wire (available from Alan Gibson) and fashion a pair of pipes as shown in **Figure 14**. Glue the pieces of wire into the holes drilled in the smokebox sides so that their longer (6mm) sections point downwards and will appear to pass through the running-plate when we unite the boiler and chassis.

The 'Austin Sevens' had two mechanical lubricators, one on each side of the locomotive. White-metal castings for LMS-pattern

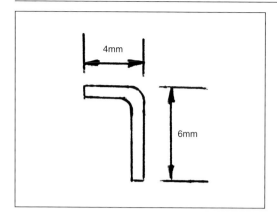

Figure 14: New front steam pipes

lubricators are available from many sources including South Eastern Finecast, Jackson-Evans and Comet Models. On this model I used the South Eastern Finecast variety. The lubricators sit on the running-plate 28mm from its leading edge, one on each side of the locomotive.

Now fit the whistle into the rearmost of the three holes in the top of the firebox (I used a whistle from a Hornby 'B17'). Also fit the two safety-valves (I re-used the ones from the 'Patriot'). Next fit the boiler handrails; again I refitted the rails from the 'Patriot' (suitably shortened, of course).

The firebox/boiler/smokebox assembly can now be glued to the running-plate and cab. The 'Austin Sevens', in common with most other Fowler designs, had a rectangular box in front of the cab on the driver's (left-hand) side of the loco. Manufacture this box from a 16mm length of 2.5mm-square microstrip, round off the top

leading edge with a file (use photographs as a guide) and glue in place. Next fashion a reversing-rod from 1mm-square microstrip, or a length of 1mm-wide scrap brass (**Figure 15**). Glue it to the left-hand side of the loco with its rear end butting up against the leading edge of the firebox, halfway between the running-plate and the boiler handrail. The leading end of the reversing-rod should now rest on the running-plate just ahead of the front steps.

Stage 3: The tender

The tender from the Hornby 'Patriot' is an interesting creation; it has a lot of fine detail but is 4mm too long and 5mm too wide. One could invoke a bit of 'modeller's licence' and make do with the existing body, but it is noticeably wider than the 4F cab! I decided to build a new tender body from card to achieve something closer to the required width, although there was nothing I could do about the length.

The Hornby plastic body is held in place by two lugs on each side of the tender frame, and these need to be cut or filed away. Manufacture the new tender sides and rear from card (**Figure 16**), then pierce holes in the sides with a safety-pin to accommodate the handrails (**Figure 17**). Next cut out a rectangular piece of card 30mm by 20mm and glue it to the inside edges of the tender sides 7mm from the leading edges, thus forming the tender front. When the glue has set, giving us a more stable four-sided structure, fit the four handrails. The two front handrails can be assembled in the normal way with handrail knobs; however, the rear handrails will be too

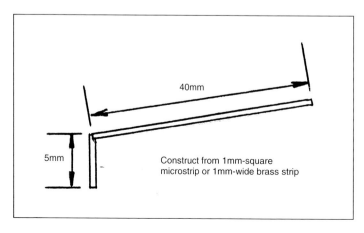

Construct from 1mm-square microstrip or 1mm-wide brass strip

Figure 15: New reversing-rod

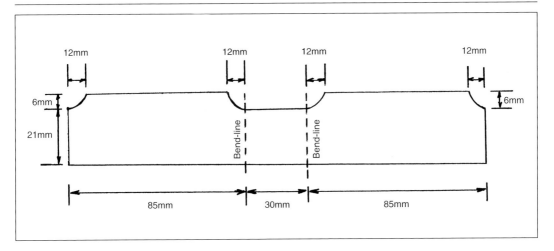

Figure 16: Manufacture of new sides and rear for tender

Figure 17: Position of tender handrails

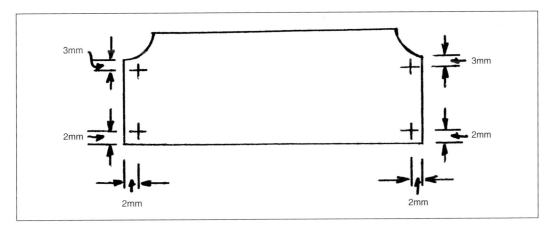

close to the rear weight to be able to use handrail knobs; I just threaded the 0.7mm-diameter wire through the holes and bent over the ends on the inside with pliers.

The remainder of the tender construction is best carried out with the card body sitting in place over the mechanism. Cut out a rectangular piece of card 29mm by 20mm to form the top of the water tank. Pierce holes in the card to fit the dome and water-filler (**Figure 18**), then fit the two castings; white-metal castings for both these items are available from Comet Models, South Eastern Finecast and Jackson-Evans (from their 4F tender kits). With the castings in place, glue the tank top to the rear of the tender body with its underside resting on top of the rear weight. Manufacture the two coal partitions as shown in

Figure 19, and glue them in position, the front one in the angles between the top edges and the front cut-outs (use photographs as a guide), while the rear one forms an angle of 90° with the top of the water tank.

Next cut out a rectangular piece of card 30mm by 5mm and glue it in place between the tender front and the front coal partition, thus forming a horizontal shelf. Cut out a rectangular piece of 80-thou Plasticard 30mm by 9mm to form the footplate. Drill two 1mm-diameter holes on the transverse centre-line 4mm in from each outside edge to take the handles for the brake and water-scoop; white-metal castings for these are again available from Comet Models, Jackson-Evans and South Eastern Finecast (from their 4F tender kits). With these two castings fitted in place,

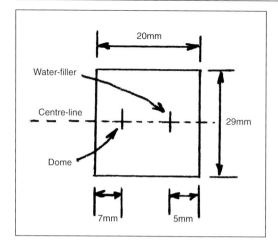

Figure 18: Top of water tank

Figure 19: Front and rear coal partitions

glue the footplate in position at the front of the tender 5mm above the bottom edges. Next manufacture a top for the coal space (again from card), as shown in **Figure 20**. Pierce four holes through this to take the tender-vents and fire-iron brackets; white-metal castings for the tender-vents are available from Comet Models and Jackson-Evans, and a white-metal casting for the fire-iron bracket is available from South Eastern Finecast. With the castings in place, glue the coal space top between the two coal partitions so as to cover the power unit. When the glue has dried cover the top of the coal space with coal.

We now need a couple of steps on the rear of the tender. These can be made from rectangles of card or 1mm-thick Plasticard 2mm square and glued in place halfway up, 2mm in from the outside edge. Fine etched-brass lamp-brackets and etched-brass LMS maker's plates are available from South Eastern Finecast (from their 4F tender kit). At this point the more enterprising loco-builder may wish to add more detail at the front end – lockers, coal-chute, fire-irons, etc. If you wish to model one of the locos with tender coal-rails a set of etched-brass coal-rails is available from Craftsman Models, Alan Gibson, South Eastern Finecast and Jackson-

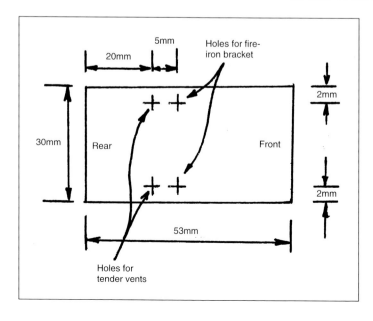

Figure 20: Top for coal space

The completed tender

Evans. Please note that if you decide to fit your model with coal-rails you will have to put the tender-vents at the rear of the tender, located on either side of the water-dome (consult photographs for guidance).

The model is now ready for painting and transfers. The livery carried in BR days was unlined black. The BR power classification was 7F and all locomotives carried this above the cab-side numbers. This is another useful and unusual locomotive that would be at home on any ex-LMS layout, and wouldn't be out of place on layouts set on other Regions, working on an inter-regional freight.

Ex-CR 2F 'Jumbo' 0-6-0 No 57345

The Caledonian Railway introduced its '294' Class of 0-6-0 freight locomotives in 1883. They were designed by Dugald Drummond and employed 5ft 0in-diameter driving wheels, two inside cylinders 18 inches in diameter, a 150psi boiler with a round-top firebox, and Ramsbottom safety-valves mounted on the top of the steam-dome. The tenders were originally fitted with under-hung springs, ie fitted *below* the axleboxes, but these were replaced by the conventional type (above the axleboxes) from 1894 onwards. A total of 163 examples were built between 1883 and 1895; 35 were built by Neilson & Co Ltd of Glasgow, the remainder being built at the Caledonian Railway's own workshops at St Rollox. While the majority of the class had steam-brakes only, 22 were equipped with Westinghouse brakes, and one loco was dual-braked (Westinghouse and vacuum).

Dugald Drummond left the Caledonian in 1890 for 'greener pastures' with the London & South Western Railway. In 1895 one of his successors, J. F. McIntosh, introduced his '711' Class, which were identical to Drummond's design apart from being fitted with conventional tender springs, Westinghouse brakes, and Ramsbottom safety-valves mounted (more conventionally) atop the firebox. A total of 81 of these locos were built between 1895 and 1897. Five were fitted with condensing apparatus for working on the Glasgow low-level suburban lines; however, this equipment was removed by the LMS shortly after the Grouping. Concurrent with the construction of the '711' Class McIntosh converted all 163 members of the '294' Class into '711s', eventually making a class of 244 locomotives. Because of their superior hauling power compared to previous Caledonian

designs, these locos were given the nickname 'Jumbos' by their crews. Twenty-five members of the class were commandeered for war service during the First World War; they all survived and were returned to the Caledonian in 1919.

All 244 locomotives survived to become LMS property in 1923. Both the '294' and '711' Classes originally had boiler-side clack-valves, but these were moved inside the cabs in LMS days. The LMS also replaced the Ramsbottom safety-valves with the more modern Ross 'pop' variety during the 1930s. During their period of ownership the LMS fitted dual brakes (Westinghouse and vacuum) to a large proportion of the class; however, after the Second World War the Westinghouse braking equipment was removed from some of them. In the 1930s a small number of the locos were tried out in the Leeds district, but they proved unpopular with the crews (the 'Midland' men would have been used to firing Belpaire fireboxes and a round-top firebox required different firing techniques), so they were quickly returned to Scotland! More successful was the transfer of some of the locos to former Glasgow & South Western Railway and Highland Railway territory, where they remained until final withdrawal. The locos transferred to the former Highland lines were subsequently fitted with tender cabs to provide extra protection from severe weather conditions.

Five members of the class were withdrawn prior to nationalisation (the first in March 1946), leaving 239 examples to become BR property in 1948. Withdrawals continued steadily, however, until the class was rendered extinct in November 1963 with the condemnation of the last five locos (Nos 57261, 57270, 57309, 57355 and 57375). This is

Above 'Jumbo' 0-6-0 No 57396, one of the Westinghouse-braked examples, stands at Stirling South shed on 31 July 1956. *David Holmes*

Below The model of No 57345. Note the Westinghouse pump on the right-hand side of the firebox, the (as yet unpainted) reversing rod on the left-hand side of the loco, and the Caledonian-style lamp-brackets on the side of the cab. The fire-irons are by Springside, and the transfers are a mixture of SMS, Fox and Modelmaster.

certainly another class worthy of modelling, being numerous (244 examples) and long-lived (80 years!). They were also widespread, certainly in Scotland, and class members could be seen in Carlisle, Stranraer, Dundee, Aberdeen, Oban, Wick and Thurso. A model would be a useful addition to any Scottish-based layout.

Modelling notes

Because of the large number of possible permutations – types of chimney, dome and braking systems – the loco-builder is advised to work from a photograph of his chosen subject.

1 In spite of their early vintage, all members of the class were left-hand drive (with the reversing rod on the left-hand side).

2 Some locos were dual-braked, carrying a Westinghouse pump on their right-hand side, a vacuum-ejector pipe on the left-hand side of the boiler, and two brake-pipe hoses on the buffer beams. Some had the Westinghouse brake only, carrying a Westinghouse pump on the right-hand side and one brake-pipe hose on each buffer-beam. Some locos were vacuum-braked only, carrying a vacuum-ejector pipe along the left-hand side of the boiler and one brake-pipe hose on each buffer-beam.

3 Some locos carried the standard Caledonian-pattern chimney, while others carried an LMS tapered stovepipe chimney.

4 Most locos carried the standard Caledonian-pattern round-topped steam dome, while others carried a dome with a squared top (fitted in LMS days).

5 All locos were fitted with Ross 'pop' safety-valves (on a circular base) in LMS days.

6 Originally the '294' Class had brake-rodding fitted outside the driving wheels; however, this was repositioned between the wheels by the LMS during the 1920s.

Items required

Hornby/Dapol 'Dean Goods' loco body and chassis; Hornby/Dapol LMS 4F tender chassis and power unit; detailing parts described in the text.

Stage 1: The loco and tender chassis

The only modification that needs to be carried out on the loco chassis is the removal of the outside brake-rodding (however, even this is unnecessary if your model is to operate on a pre-Grouping layout). The plastic brake-rodding is

The underside of the model showing how the 'Dean Goods' drawbar engages with the 6BA bolt.

only a 'clip-fit' so can be easily lifted off with a penknife blade. Fit a 6BA nut and bolt through the hole in the front of the tender chassis formerly occupied by the tender body fixing-screw.

At this stage it would be a good idea to solder the electrical leads from the loco current-collectors to the terminals on the 4F power unit. To couple the loco and tender together use the tender drawbar from the 'Dean Goods' in conjunction with the previously mentioned 6BA nut and bolt.

Stage 2: The loco body

Begin the dissection of the loco body with the removal of the front sandboxes, the vacuum brake-pipe and the cab (these are only a 'clip-fit' so a penknife blade should lift them off). Then remove the metal body weight (held in place by a screw on the underside of the boiler). Using a craft-knife, remove the reversing-rod, then remove the chimney, the dome and the GWR-pattern vacuum-ejector pipe (on the right-hand side of the smokebox, just above the handrail). If your model is to be one of the locos fitted with a

'wheel and handle' smokebox door fastening you will need to remove the 'twin handle' fastening (this is best achieved with a craft-knife). Next remove the top of the Belpaire firebox with a vertical hacksaw cut immediately behind the fourth boiler-band, and two further cuts angled downwards and outwards on either side of the firebox just below the boiler handrail (**Figure 1**). Be careful not to damage the boiler handrails.

Next fabricate a new (round) top for the firebox from a piece of card 18mm by 25mm, bend the card to match the profile of the boiler and try in position. If it is too long, trim it until a satisfactory fit is obtained, then glue in place. When the glue has dried, take a piece of paper 19mm by 35mm and glue it over the new firebox top, to cover the joins and hide the 'threepenny-bit effect' (**Figures 2 and 3**).

The removal of the steam-dome will have left a 'recess' in the top of the boiler, so fill this with Milliput or similar; at the same time, fill in the four small holes in the top of the boiler. When the filler has set, file flush with the surface of the boiler. Pierce a hole through the top of the firebox 3mm from the rear edge of the firebox on the longitudinal centre-line, to take the whistle.

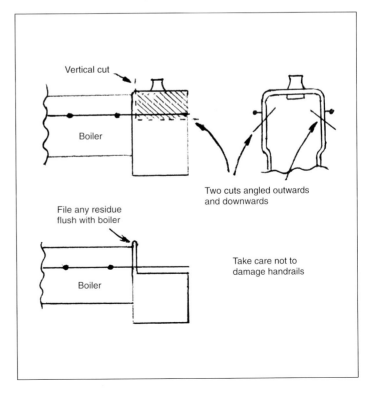

Figure 1: Removal of Belpaire firebox

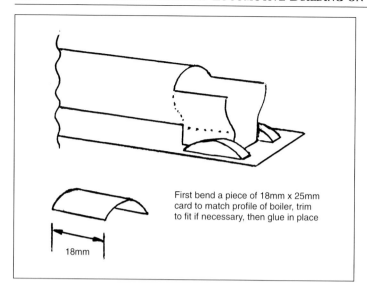

First bend a piece of 18mm x 25mm card to match profile of boiler, trim to fit if necessary, then glue in place

18mm

Figure 2: Construction of round-topped firebox: step one

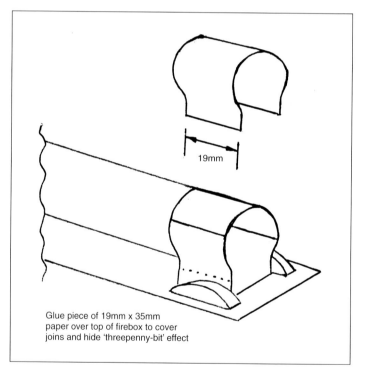

19mm

Glue piece of 19mm x 35mm paper over top of firebox to cover joins and hide 'threepenny-bit' effect

Figure 3: Construction of round-topped firebox: step two

Next replace the metal weight inside the boiler. With this securely in place we can turn our attention to the construction of a new cab. First, from card or thin Plasticard, manufacture a new cab front as shown in **Figure 4** and glue it in place. Then manufacture a pair of cab sides (**Figure 5**) and glue them in place. More enterprising loco-builders may at this stage wish to add a certain amount of interior detail depending on personal preference – cab floor, boiler backhead, seats, etc. Next manufacture the cab rear handrails from 1mm-diameter brass wire (available from Alan Gibson) as shown in **Figure 6**, and glue them to the rear of the cab. With this done, cut out a rectangle of card 23mm long by 32mm wide to form the cab roof, bend it to shape and glue it in place.

We now turn our attention to the cab roof

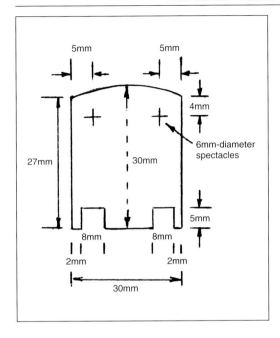

Figure 4: New cab front

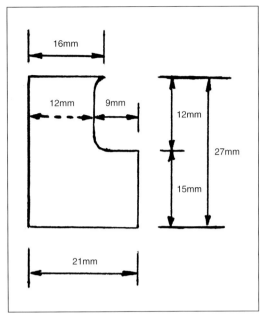

Figure 5: New cab sides

Figure 6: Cab rear handrails

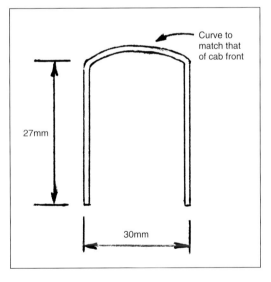

ribs, manufactured from 1mm-square microstrip. First cut two 23mm lengths and glue them to the sides of the cab roof along the outside edges. Then cut three 30mm lengths to form the transverse ribs; glue one to the leading edge of the roof, another to the rear edge, and the third along the transverse centre-line. At this point it would be a good idea to paint the cab (both inside and out) and the firebox. Next manufacture the combined front splashers and sandboxes from card (**Figure 7**) – note that the assembly includes the smokebox wing-plates – and glue them in place.

We now move on to the smokebox door handle. If you are modelling one of the locos with a wheel and handle fastening, a suitable white-metal casting is available from South Eastern Finecast. In order to fit the casting you will need to drill a 1mm-diameter hole through the centre of the smokebox door. To accommodate the lamp-brackets, first drill three 1mm-diameter holes through the running-plate above the buffer-beam, one directly above the front coupling and the other two directly above each buffer. Etched-brass lamp-brackets are available from South-Eastern Finecast and Westward Models. Fit one of these into each drilled hole. For the top lamp-bracket I used a

piece of scrap brass 2mm wide by 10mm long, bent it into an 'L' shape and glued it to the top of the smokebox. All Caledonian locomotives (or at least the ones that worked on the main lines) carried two extra lamp-brackets, one on each side of the cab approximately halfway between the driver's cut-out and the cab front at roughly the same level as the front spectacles.

If you are modelling one of the locomotives

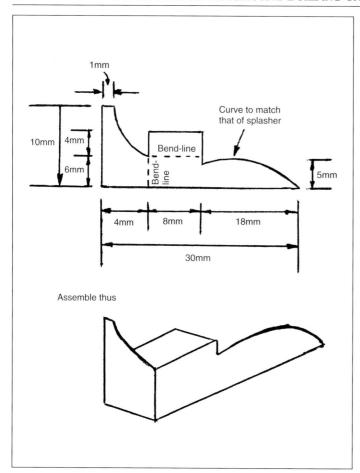

Figure 7: Combined splashers and front sand-boxes

Below The front and rear of the finished model. At the front the smokebox wing-plates are just visible, as are the etched-brass spectacle surrounds. The lamp-brackets are from Westward and the numberplate and shedplate are SMS transfers. The rear lamp-brackets are from South Eastern Finecast.

fitted with the Westinghouse brake, you will need to glue a Westinghouse pump to the right-hand side of the firebox halfway between the front of the cab and the centre splasher with its base sitting on the running-plate. Suitable white-metal castings for these pumps are available from many sources including Westward Products, Dave Alexander, Jackson-Evans, and South Eastern Finecast. On my model I used a casting from the last-mentioned. Likewise, if you are modelling one of the locomotives fitted with the vacuum brake, you will need to fit a vacuum-ejector pipe along the left-hand side of the boiler. This pipe will need to run from the cab to a point midway along the smokebox, 2mm above the handrail. At the time of writing suitable plastic mouldings (from the Hornby 'A3') are obtainable from Modelspares and East Kent Models; failing this one could use a length of 1mm-diameter brass wire (available from Alan Gibson).

Next, from a piece of scrap brass or 1mm-square microstrip, manufacture a reversing-rod. This will need to be 1mm wide by 22mm long, and runs from the leading edge of the firebox to a point on the running-plate midway between the centre and leading splashers on the left-hand side of the locomotive. Refer to photographs for the shape and profile of this item. If your chosen model was fitted with train brakes you will need to glue a brake-pipe to the front buffer-beam, and if your model is a dual-braked example it will need two brake-pipes on each buffer-beam.

We now move on to the boiler mountings. As regards the whistle, re-use one of the whistles from the 'Dean Goods' and glue it into the hole in the top of the firebox made earlier. Suitable white-metal castings for chimney, dome and safety-valves (including both varieties of dome and chimney) are available from South Eastern Finecast (from their 'Caledonian tank' loco kit). Glue the safety-valve casting to the top of the firebox astride the longitudinal centre-line and 10mm from the front of the cab. The chimney and dome need to be glued in the same positions as their GWR predecessors. Finally, Jackson-Evans produce a pair of etched-brass 6mm-diameter spectacle surrounds (item number G.61 in their range); glue a pair of these over the cab-front spectacles.

Stage 3: The tender body

First manufacture a new tender body from card, pierce eight holes to take the handrails, and bend along the broken lines (**Figure 8**). Then fit the handrails; the rear handrails are so close to the tender weight that it is not possible to fit conventional handrail knobs. On my model I used two lengths of 0.7mm-diameter brass wire (obtainable from Alan Gibson) threaded through the holes with the ends bent over on the inside. However, the front handrails can be fitted in the conventional way.

Next manufacture a new tender front (**Figure**

Figure 8: New tender body

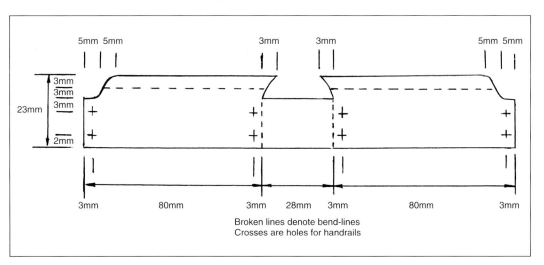

Broken lines denote bend-lines
Crosses are holes for handrails

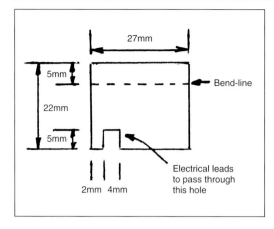

Figure 9: New tender front

Figure 10: New top for rear of tender

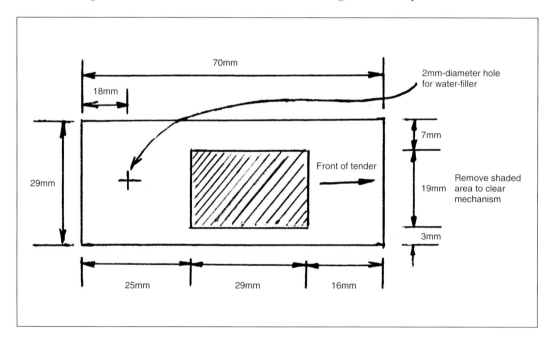

Figure 11: New top for coal and water space

9) and glue it in place at the front of the main portion of the body 5mm from the leading edges, with the top 5mm bent over rearwards to form a shelf (to take the lockers/toolboxes). Then manufacture a new top for the rear of the tender (**Figure 10**) and bend it to match the rear of the main portion of the body, thus giving us a flared top when it is glued in place.

Cut out a rectangle of card 25mm by 20mm and glue it to the inside of the tender rear with its bottom edge level with that of the main portion of the body. Then cut out two rectangles

of card 65mm by 20mm and glue them to the inside of the tender sides, again with their bottom edges level with those of the tender body (these will support the top of the coal and water space). Next manufacture a new top for the coal and water space from card (**Figure 11**), and glue in place.

Glue the lockers/toolboxes to the 5mm-wide shelf at the front of the tender; suitable white-metal castings for these are available from South Eastern Finecast (from their 'J69' loco kit). With this done, manufacture a front coal partition from card (**Figure 12**) and glue it to the rear of the lockers/toolboxes. Next manufacture the rear coal partition, again from card (**Figure 13**), and glue in position 55mm to the rear of the front partition. Then manufacture the tender footplate from card or Plasticard (**Figure 14**). With this done fit the tender brake handle. White-metal castings for these are available from many sources; I used a white-metal casting from South Eastern Finecast (from their 4F kit). Then fit the assembled footplate to the front of the tender 5mm above the bottom edge.

Next fit the water-filler; again these are available from many sources, and on my model I used a brass casting from Westward Model Products (item number M.017 in their range). Then cut out a rectangle of paper 40mm by 25mm, and (with the tender body sitting over the mechanism) glue it to the top of the coal space to cover the top of the mechanism. When the glue has dried cover the coal space with imitation coal.

Now is a good time to paint the model. The livery carried in BR days was unlined black. When the paint has dried glue four lamp-brackets to the rear of the tender and, depending on the identity of your model, fit one or two brake-pipes to the tender buffer-beam as necessary. With this done your model is now ready for the application of transfers. The BR power classification was 2F and this was carried by all locos above the fleet number on the cab side. Finally, glue a set of Springside fire-irons to the top of the coal and your model is complete, providing a useful and unusual addition to any Scottish-based layout.

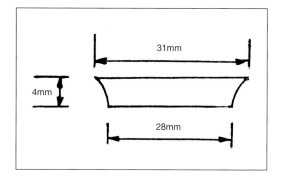

Figure 12: Front coal partition

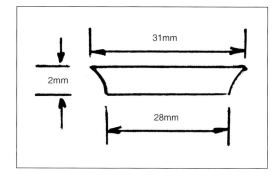

Figure 13: Rear coal partition

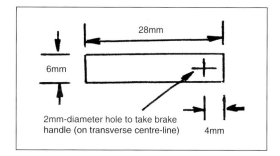

Figure 14: Tender footplate

Ex-M&SWJR 2-4-0 No 1335

In 1873 a new railway was mooted to link Swindon with the London & South Western Railway at Andover as a first step towards linking Andover with the Midland Railway at Cheltenham Spa. The Midland looked favourably upon this venture as it would give it access to Southampton. The LSWR was also favourable as it would give that company access to traffic to and from the Midlands and the North of England (via the Midland Railway). The new line, entitled the 'Swindon, Marlborough & Andover Railway', was opened in February 1883, and almost immediately work began on the construction of the 'Swindon & Cheltenham Extension Railway' with the intention of linking Swindon with Andoversford on the Great Western Railway's Oxford to Cheltenham line (access to Cheltenham being achieved by running powers over the GWR). These running powers were duly granted by Parliament, much to the annoyance of the GWR, and over the ensuing years the Midland & South Western Junction Railway, as it was now entitled, was perpetually a thorn in the Great Western's side.

Through services to the Midland Railway station at Cheltenham Spa (Lansdown) began on 1 August 1891. The M&SWJR led a precarious existence, being 'bailed out' on a number of occasions by its two larger partners. However, unlike the Somerset & Dorset, the M&SWJR retained its independence with its own rolling-stock and small loco fleet (all constructed by private builders). In 1894 the Glasgow firm of Dubs & Co constructed three small 2-4-0 tender locomotives for working passenger trains on the line. These locos employed 150psi boilers, round-top fireboxes, Ramsbottom safety-valves, two inside cylinders

(17 by 24 inches) and 5ft 6in-diameter driving wheels.

In spite of the LSWR and Midland interest in the line, somehow the GWR gained control of it at the 1923 Grouping. However, the history books quote a date of 29 October 1923 for the GWR takeover (not 1 January, as was the case with the rest of the 'grouped' companies). This was due to a dispute with the Midland Railway's successor, the LMS, resulting in the GWR giving the LMS £85,000 worth of shares in compensation – the LMS had originally claimed a quarter of a million!

Almost straightaway the GWR began rebuilding all of its absorbed locomotives. The three M&SWJR 2-4-0s were all rebuilt with 165psi Dean parallel boilers and Belpaire fireboxes during 1924, and were allocated the GWR numbers 1334, 1335 and 1336. Later they were transferred to Reading (Nos 1335 and 1336) and Didcot (No 1334) where they operated local trains on the Reading-Didcot-Newbury triangle. All three survived to become BR property in 1948, and one of their last regular duties was the pick-up goods on the Newbury to Lambourne branch. Nos 1334 and 1335 were both condemned in September 1952, with No 1336 following in March 1954.

As to the line itself, right from the beginning of its ownership the GWR began to run it down; it was singled throughout its length (apart from passing-loops at major stations) by the early 1930s. This policy was continued by the GWR's successor, BR (Western Region), and when the WR gained control of the ex-LMS territory south of Birmingham in the early 1950s this run-down gained momentum. By the end of the 1950s through passenger services on the route were down to one train per day in each direction,

Above In the last year of its life, ex-M&SWJR 2-4-0 No 1335, still with a faint 'GWR' on its tender, stands at Reading on 2 March 1952. *John Edgington*

Below The completed model of No 1335. The MJT wagon springs are just visible above the leading axle. The transfers are from Modelmaster, and the numberplates from Guilplates Ltd.

a through working from Southampton (Terminus) to Cheltenham Spa and return. The WR closed the line to both passenger and freight traffic on 9 September 1961.

The M&SWJR must have been a very interesting line, and given the fact that ex-LMS and Southern locos traversed the line daily and could be seen side by side with the 'native' ex-GWR locos, it would be an interesting subject for a layout. The LSWR running powers were inherited by the Southern Railway, and in turn by BR (Southern Region), which brought 'T9s', 'Black Motors' and SR 'Moguls' regularly on to the line. The appearance of a Southern loco at Cheltenham Spa was a daily occurrence (this must have been the furthest north that Southern locos ventured on a regular basis).

As for the trio of 2-4-0s, a 60-year life-span for such a small class was quite an achievement, and one of these locos would be an unusual addition to any GWR or South Western Division layout.

Historical notes were compiled with the assistance of *The Midland & South Western Junction Railway* by David Bartholomew (Wild Swan Publications Ltd).

Items required

Hornby or Dapol 'Dean Goods' loco body and chassis; Hornby 'Patriot' power unit; Hornby 'B12' tender chassis frame; three small Hornby wagon weights; two 6BA screws, one 10BA nut and bolt, and one 4BA washer; detailing parts as described in the text.

Stage 1: The loco chassis

Begin the conversion by removing the front coupling-rods from each side of the chassis, together with the leading pair of driving wheels and their axle. Then drill a 1.5mm-diameter hole through the chassis, in line with the original axle-hole but 3mm lower. Solder a piece of 1mm-diameter brass wire (available from Alan Gibson), 8mm long, to the leading current-collectors on each side of the chassis;

The completed 2-4-0 chassis. The additional wiring to collect current from the leading wheels is just visible.

this will enable the current to be collected via the leading wheels. Next fit a pair of 13mm-diameter bogie-wheels through the newly drilled hole, while at the same time ensuring that the newly added pieces of wire are in contact with the inside of the leading wheels. Test for contact with the rails; if the new wheels are too high, enlarge the hole until they do come into contact with the rails. With this done your chassis is now complete and you have created a 2-4-0!

Stage 2: The loco body

First remove the cab with a penknife blade, then remove the front sandboxes, again using a penknife blade. Remove the front splashers with a craft-knife (take care not to damage the short handrails above the front steps). Then drill four 1mm-diameter holes to take the front lamp-brackets, one through the top of the running-plate above the front coupling-hook, another through the top of the smokebox immediately in front of the chimney on the centre-line (take care not to damage the chimney), and two more through the top of the running-plate above each buffer.

The removal of the front splashers will have left a hole in each side of the smokebox saddle, so fill these with Milliput or similar. Their removal will also have left two rectangular holes

in the running-plate – cover these with rectangles of paper. We now need to fit a couple of front axle springs to the running-plate, with their centres 20mm from the front buffer-beam (on my model I used a pair of MJT wagon springs).

We now turn our attention to the manufacture of a new cab. First, from card or thin Plasticard, fabricate a new cab front (**Figure 1**) and glue it in place. Then manufacture, again from card or thin Plasticard, a pair of new cab sides (**Figure 2**). Next fabricate the two cab-side handrails from 0.7mm-diameter brass wire (available from Alan Gibson), and fix them to the cab sides by bending over the ends on the inside. With this done, glue the cab sides in place.

Next manufacture the cab rear handrails from 0.9mm brass wire (Alan Gibson) (**Figure 3**), and glue them to the rear of the cab sides (with the top corners of the wire on the inside of the cab). Then manufacture a new cab roof from card (**Figure 4**), bend it to shape and glue it in place, using the top of the rear handrails to support the rear of the cab. When the glue has dried fit the whistles (from the 'Dean Goods') into the two holes in the cab roof (see **Figure 4**). With this done you can now fit the lamp-brackets; etched-brass lamp-brackets are available from South Eastern Finecast and Westward Model Products.

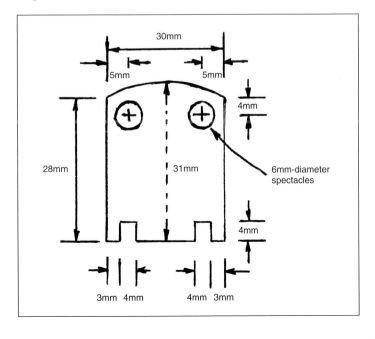

Figure 1: New cab front

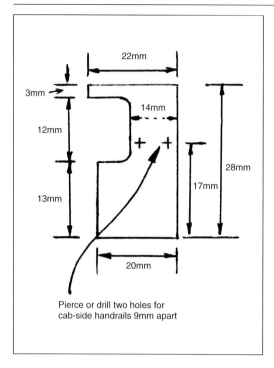

Figure 2: New cab sides

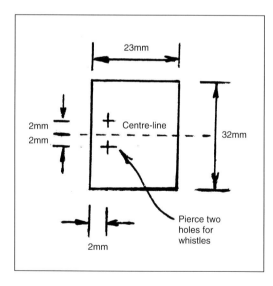

Figure 4: New cab roof

Fit a vacuum brake-pipe to the front buffer-beam and your loco is ready for painting and numbering. At this point you may wish to add a cab interior – backhead, seats and crew. A suitable white-metal casting for a boiler backhead is available from South Eastern Finecast (from their 4F loco kit).

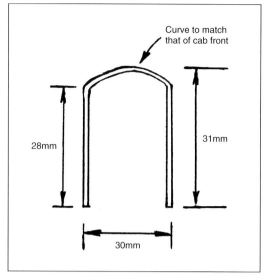

Figure 3: Cab rear handrails

Stage 3: The power unit and tender chassis

First, with a craft-knife or hacksaw blade, remove sufficient material from the 'B12' tender underframe to clear the motor housing and gears of the 'Patriot' power unit (**Figure 5**). Drill a 3mm-diameter hole through the top of the tender frame on the longitudinal centre-line, 12mm from the front edge, followed by a 2mm-diameter hole 3mm from the front edge (again see **Figure 5**). Next remove the wheels from the front (stepped) end of the power unit and remove the step with a hacksaw. Replace the front wheels, then remove the rear wheels and remove 3mm from the rear end of the power unit (**Figure 6**). Test-fit the power unit to the tender frame and *make sure that the rear wheels are clear of the coupling.*

Next, with the power unit in place inside the tender-frame, fit a 6BA screw into the 3mm-diameter hole that you drilled through the top of the tender frame. Then take a second 6BA screw and a 4BA washer and insert them into the hole at the rear of the power unit; you will find that the washer overlaps the edge of the tender frame and holds the power unit and frame firmly together. Next fit a 15mm-long 10BA nut and bolt through the 2mm diameter hole that you drilled through the front of the tender-frame;

Figure 5: Modifications to 'B12' tender underframe

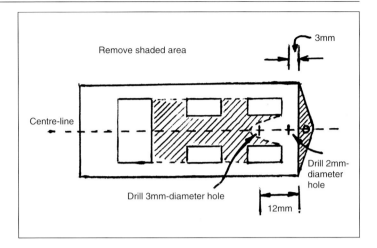

Figure 6: Modifications to 'Patriot' power unit

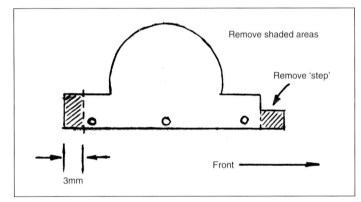

The completed tender chassis, showing the soldered leads and the two 6BA screws holding the chassis and power unit together (note the 4BA washer). Also visible is the 10BA nut and bolt that connect with the 'Dean Goods' drawbar.

The underside of the chassis. Note how the 10BA bolt engages with the 'Dean Goods' drawbar.

this will fit into the drawbar of the locomotive.

We can now solder the ends of the pick-up wires to the terminals of the power unit and test-run it on the layout; if it short-circuits swap the leads over and try again.

Stage 4: The tender body

First fabricate the new sides and rear from card (**Figure 7**), then pierce holes for the handrails (**Figure 8**); for the latter I used 0.7mm-diameter brass wire (from Alan Gibson). After fitting the handrails, bend the new body to the required shape, paying particular attention to the flared top (use photographs as a guide to the required profile).

Manufacture a new tender front from card (**Figure 9**) and bend over the top 5mm to form a horizontal shelf (to accommodate the toolboxes). The cut-out at the bottom corner is to fit over the electrical leads, so it needs to be on the same side as the terminals.

With the tender front securely glued in place, giving us a more stable assembly to work on, we can turn our attention to the subject of weights. While there is not much room to spare inside the tender body, I was able to fit a Hornby wagon weight along the inside edge of each tender side. These weights measure 43mm by 12mm and are 3mm thick, and are currently available from Modelspares and East Kent Models. I also took a third weight, sawed it in half transversely with a

Figure 7: New tender body

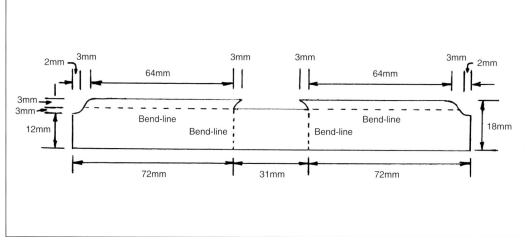

Figure 8: Position of handrails

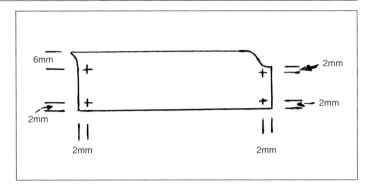

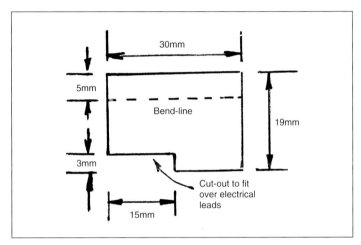

Figure 9: New tender front

The underside of the tender body, showing the wagon weights glued in place.

hacksaw, and glued the two halves together side by side. Once the glue had dried I glued the assembly to the inside of the tender rear. A useful tip is to fix the three weights at the same height, thus providing a platform on which the top of the coal and water space can rest. Finally cover the metal weight adjacent to the electrical leads with insulating-tape, paper or masking-tape to prevent short-circuits.

Next manufacture a new top for the coal and water space from card or thin Plasticard (**Figure 10**), and glue it in place resting on the tops of the previously mentioned wagon weights. With the new top in place, manufacture a new tender rear from card (**Figure 11**). Bend it to shape (using photographs as a guide) and glue in place.

That done, glue a pair of toolboxes on to the front shelf; suitable white-metal castings are

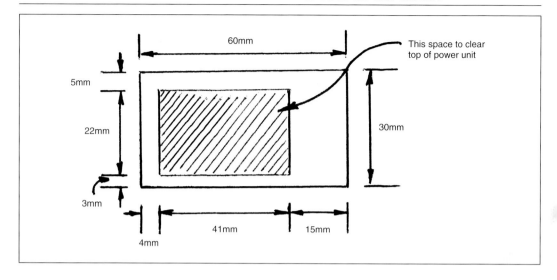

Figure 10: New top for coal and water space

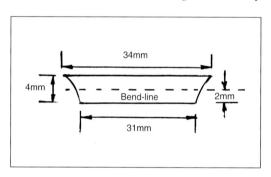

Figure 11: New tender rear

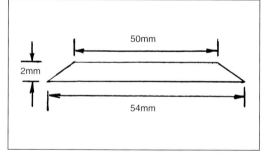

Figure 12: Front coal partition

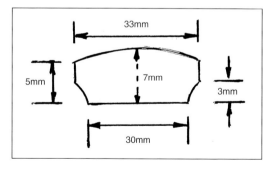

Figure 13: Rear coal partition

Figure 14: New tender side-raves

available from South Eastern Finecast (from their LNER 'J69' loco kit). Next manufacture the front coal partition from card (**Figure 12**) and glue it to the rear of the pair of toolboxes. Manufacture the rear coal partition as shown in **Figure 13** and glue it in position 50mm to the rear of the front partition. Then cut out a rectangle of paper approximately 50mm by 35mm to cover the top of the coal space and power unit; this is a fiddly job involving a lot of trial and error, and a lot of folding and trimming, but I can't think of any alternative method. When the glue has dried paint the paper cover black, then cover with imitation coal.

Another view of 2-4-0 No 1335 on an SLS special along the Shipston-on-Stour branch on 31 August 1952. The loco was withdrawn the following month, and the branch, having lost its passenger service in 1929, closed to goods traffic in May 1960. *John Edgington*

Next manufacture a pair of new side-raves from card (**Figure 14**) and glue them to the upper (exposed) portions of the coal partitions (use photographs as a guide to their positioning). Glue a water-filler to the exact centre of the top of the water space; a suitable white-metal casting is available from South Eastern Finecast (from their SR 'Mogul' loco kit). This is the moment to add more detail to the front of the tender if desired – footplate, coal-chute and brake-handle. Next fit a vacuum brake-pipe to the rear buffer-beam.

The model can now be painted. The livery carried during GWR days was unlined Brunswick green, replaced by unlined black in BR days. When the paint has dried fit four lamp-brackets to the rear of the tender; etched-brass lamp-brackets are available from Westward Model Products and South Eastern Finecast. The model is now ready for transfers and numberplates; etched-brass numberplates for all three members of this class are available from Guilplates Ltd. As far as I can ascertain these locos were unrestricted as regards route availability; so they did not carry GW-style coloured spots. With the three wagon weights providing adhesion in the tender, my model can haul four Hornby Mark 1 coaches or ten short-wheelbase goods wagons.

USEFUL ADDRESSES

Dave Alexander Models
37 Glanton Road
North Shields
Northumberland
NE29 8LJ
Tel: 0191 257 6716

Antex Electronics Ltd
2 Westbridge Industrial Estate
Tavistock
Devon
PL19 8DE
Tel: 01822 613565
(Soldering-iron manufacturers)

Bachmann Industries (Europe) Ltd
Service Department
Moat Way
Barwell
Leicestershire
LE9 8EY
Tel: 0870 751 9990

Dave Bradwell Loco Kits
South Muirinch Cottage
Gorthleck
Inverness
IV1 2YP
Tel: 01456 486377
(Loco kits and white metal castings)

CGW Nameplates
Plas Cadfor
Llwyngwril
Gwynedd
Wales
LL37 2LA
Tel: 01341 250407

Carr's Model Products Ltd
Longridge House
Cadbury Camp Lane
Clapton-in-Gordano
Bristol
BS20 7SD
Tel: 01275 852027
(Supplier of solder, flux and scenic items)

Classic Train and Motorbus
21B George Street
Royal Leamington Spa
Warwickshire
CV31 1HA
Tel: 01926 887499
(Suppliers of Jackson-Evans detailing parts)

Comet Models
105 Mossfield Road
Kings Heath
Birmingham
B14 7JE
Tel: 05602 602188

Coopercraft Ltd
17A Barclay Road
Leytonstone
London
E11 3DQ
Tel: 0208 539 3067
(Manufacturers of the 'Mailcoach' range of
coach kits and detailing parts)

Craftsman Models
149 Landor Road
Whitnash
Royal Leamington Spa
Warwickshire
CV31 2LF
Tel: 01926 428530

DMR Products Ltd
25 Halwyn Place
Redannick
Truro
Cornwall
TR1 2LA
Tel: 01872 272325

East Kent Models
89 High Street
Whitstable
Kent
CT5 1AY
Tel: 01227 770777

Fox Transfers Ltd
4 Hill Lane Close
Markfield Industrial Estate
Markfield
Leicestershire
LE67 9PN
Tel: 01530 242801/245618

Gem Model Railways
101 Harrowden Road
Bedford
MK42 0RT
Tel: 01234 261482
(Loco kits and white metal castings)

Alan Gibson Model Products
Unit 1
The Acorn Centre
Barry Street
Oldham
Lancashire
OL1 3NE
Tel: 0161 678 1607
(Loco kits, handrail wire and detailing parts)

Guilplates Ltd
32 Wodeland Avenue
Guildford
Surrey
GU2 4JZ
Tel: 01483 565980/563156

The Hereford Model Centre
4 Commercial Road
Hereford
HR1 2BA
Tel: 01432 352809
(Have been known to 'break up' ready-to-run
locos to sell body, chassis and tender separately.
Worth a try – the worse they can do is say no!)

Hornby Hobbies Ltd
Customer Service Department
Westwood
Margate
Kent
CT9 4JX
Tel: 01843 233500

Jackson-Evans
4 Dartmouth Road
Wyken
Coventry
Warwickshire
CV2 3DQ
Tel: 0247 644 3010

Little Engines
201 Cheswick Drive
Gosforth
Newcastle-upon-Tyne
Northumberland
NE3 5DS
Tel: 0191 285 9873
(Loco kits and white metal castings)

Mainly Trains Ltd
Unit 1C, South Road Workshops
South Road
Watchet
West Somerset
TA23 0HF
Tel: 01984 634543
(Loco kits, detailing parts and many other mail
order items)

Markits Ltd
PO Box 40
Watford
Hertfordshire
WD2 5TN
(Loco wheels and detailing parts)

MJT Scale Components
41 Oak Avenue
Shirley
Croydon
Surrey
CR0 8ER
(White metal detailing parts)

Modelmaster Transfers
PO Box 8560
Troon
Ayrshire
Scotland
KA10 6WX
Tel: 01292 314458

Modelspares Ltd
30 Woollam Crescent
St Albans
Herts
AL3 6EH
Tel: 01727 226203
www.modelspares.com
(Supplier of Hornby spares including bodies,
tenders, power units, etc)

Mr P. A. Paine
8 Chisholm Close
Lordshill
Southampton
Hants
SO16 8GU
Tel: 02380 739694
(Water-slide transfers made to order)

Slater's Plastikard Ltd
Royal Bank Building
Temple Road
Matlock Bath
Derbyshire
DE4 3PG
Tel: 01629 583993
(Supplier of Plasticard, microstrip and other
plastic items, plus 'Cavendish' sprung buffers)

South-Eastern Finecast Ltd
Glenn House
Hartfield Road
Forest Row
Sussex
RH18 5DZ
Tel: 01342 824711

Springside Models
2 Springside Cottages
Dornafield Road
Ipplepen
Near Newton Abbot
Devon
TQ12 5SJ
Tel: 01803 813749

W&T Manufacturing
Unit 19
Applins Farm Business Centre
Farrington
Dorset
DT11 8RA
Tel: 01747 811817
(Loco couplings, etc)

Westward Model Products
(Prop. Mr C. Parrish)
'Hillside'
Fairhead Lane
Grosmont
Nr Whitby
North Yorkshire
YO22 5PN
Tel: 01947 895373
(Loco kits and detailing parts)